THE
BREADMAN'S
HEALTHY SANDWICH
·B·O·O·K·

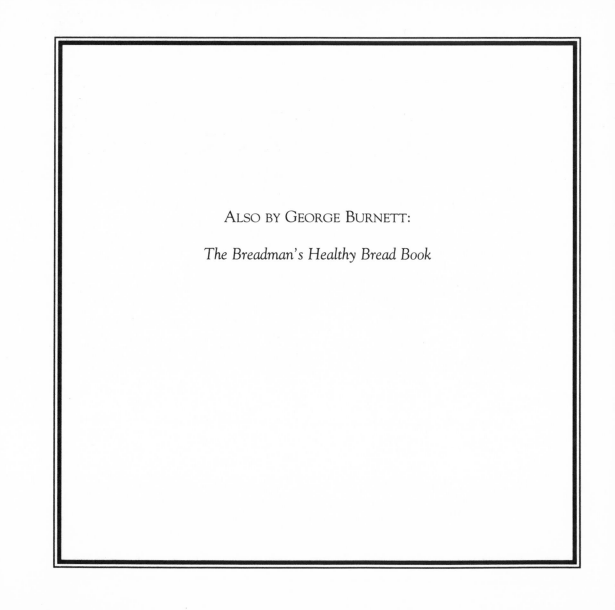

ALSO BY GEORGE BURNETT:

The Breadman's Healthy Bread Book

THE
BREADMAN'S
HEALTHY SANDWICH
·B·O·O·K·

Learn to Make More Than 55 Delicious,
Low-Fat, High-Flavor Sandwiches

George Burnett

WILLIAM MORROW AND COMPANY, INC.
New York

It is the policy of William Morrow and Company, Inc., and its imprints and affiliates, recognizing the importance of preserving what has been written, to print the books we publish on acid-free paper, and we exert our best efforts to that end.

Library of Congress Cataloging-in-Publication Data
Burnett, George.
   The breadman's healthy sandwich book : learn to make more than 55
delicious, low-fat, high-flavor sandwiches / George Burnett.
      p.   cm.
   Includes index.
   ISBN 0-688-12968-4
   1. Low-fat diet—Recipes.   2. Sandwiches.   I. Title.
RM237.7.B86   1994
641.8'4—dc20   93-21351
                                                                      CIP

Printed in the United States of America

First Edition

1 2 3 4 5 6 7 8 9 10

BOOK DESIGN BY GIORGETTA BELL McREE

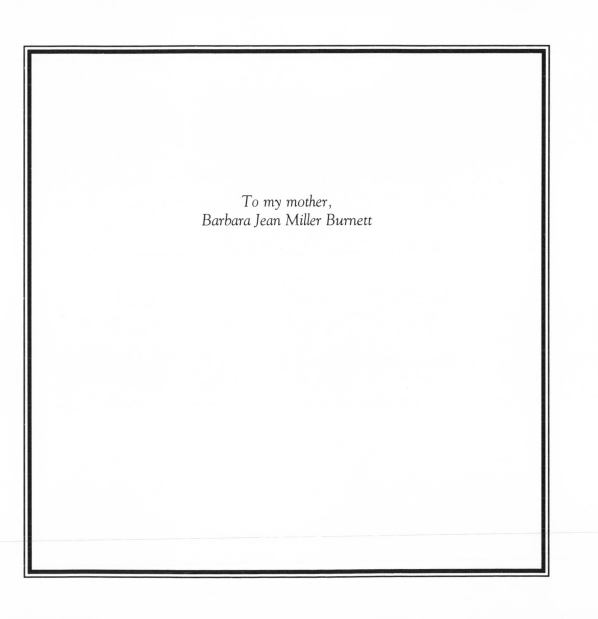

To my mother,
Barbara Jean Miller Burnett

ACKNOWLEDGMENTS

A great big Breadman thanks to all the exceptionally talented people who had a part in the development of this book.

Thanks to Will Schwalbe, my editor at William Morrow and Company, for his undaunted enthusiasm for the entire project. And thanks also to Zachary Schisgal for coordinating so much of this work.

Thanks to Mary Goodbody for her untiring efforts in assisting with the preparation of the text. Mary's sparkling personality is always so refreshing. Mary, you're terrific! And thanks to Karen Berman for editorial assistance.

Thanks to Rick Rodgers for his expertise on culinary subjects. Rick is a superstar in the food world. Thanks, Rick.

Thanks to Rick and Steve Cesari and Bob Lamson at Trillium Health Products.

A huge thanks to Bill Adler, my literary agent, for his idea of a sandwich book. And to Julie Rosner for her support.

To my father, Darwin; few if any men are more dedicated to their family. Thanks for being such a great man! And thanks for all the suggestions as you taste–tested the recipes.

Thanks to my mother, to whom this book is dedicated. Her pioneering spirit and willingness to tackle monumental projects inspires me like few others. I owe my desire for a healthy lifestyle to her. Her patient efforts to provide a nutritional upbringing for our family has been and still is appreciated. Over the years, some of these recipes were prepared by her for our family. She has worked countless hours on assisting me on this book. Mom, I love you.

Special thanks to my brothers and sisters for their support growing up and on my Breadman projects.

To the memory of Christy's parents, Eldon and Eunice Nielsen, for their constant support in my success.

Most importantly, a big hug and thanks to my sweetheart and best friend, my wife, Christy. She and our four boys, Ben, Isaac, Niel, and Matthew, are everything to me. They are my dream come true. Thanks, family.

CONTENTS

THE
BREADMAN'S
HEALTHY SANDWICH
·B·O·O·K·

Introduction

Because I am a bread baker, it comes as no surprise that I like sandwiches. After all, most bread ends up as a sandwich of some sort or another. I have followed a low-fat, whole-foods diet all my life, which explains why the sandwiches I like are not those normally served up in delis, diners, and many home kitchens across the country. Mine are full of good, wholesome foods and made with freshly baked breads. Sadly, the sandwiches most Americans eat are not especially healthful. Many are downright disgraceful!

Remember the Dagwood? It was a towering monstrosity of fatty lunch meats and cheese packed between two slices of bread that had been slathered with mayonnaise. (Should I remind you that this culinary abomination was "invented" by a cartoon character?) Or how about the super-duper hamburger special at the local fast-food joint? It's usually two beef patties, gobs of glutinous sauce, bacon, and cheese stuffed between the halves of an airy, tasteless bun.

These are the sandwiches many Americans eat, that we are *encouraged* to eat. I wrote this book to give those who want to eat healthier a variety of delicious options. Turn the pages here to find recipe after recipe for sandwiches made with fresh, healthful ingredients. Some require cooking, others don't. Most sandwich ingredients are easy to find at the supermarket, greengrocer, or natural foods store. I use fresh vegetables and herbs; canned, water-packed tuna; peanut butter; low-fat cream cheese; tomatoes; and lettuce—all familiar sandwich fare. I also use foods such as eggplant, avocados, red peppers, mushrooms, nuts, and tofu. It may surprise you to find a number of sandwiches with turkey and chicken. I rarely eat meat myself, but when I do, it is always low-fat, organic poultry. I include meat because I did not want this to be strictly a vegetarian book. I wanted to reach the optimum number of people to spread the word about healthful sandwiches and healthful eating in general, and I recognize that most folks are not vegetarians.

•

WE ARE WHAT WE EAT

I feel strongly about eating a healthful diet. You are what you eat, and if you eat high-fat, salty, and sugary foods full of empty calories, you will no doubt be overweight or courting health problems.

My family and I live in rural Montana where the air is fresh and clean and we have room to grow our own vegetables, which we love to cook. This does not mean we spend every minute in the kitchen. One evening my wife Christy and I decided to take our four young sons out for supper. We parked in front of an "all-you-can-eat" restaurant we had not been to in years. As we were leaving the car, we noticed the *size* of the customers waddling in and out of the restaurant. Without hesitation, we buckled the boys back into their seat belts and headed for our usual vegetarian restaurant.

•

A FOUNDATION OF SAND

I have an idea I call the "sand foundation" theory. When I was 18 I designed and built my own log cabin. If I had built my mountain cabin on sand rather than on a good, firm foundation, it eventually would collapse. It might stand for several years, but with the first major storm it would begin deteriorating. This is true of diet. If we eat "sand" foods—those that offer little sustenance— our bodies will begin deteriorating sooner rather than later. I believe that doctors' offices and hospitals are full of people who have built their health foundations on sand foods. These foods can be tolerated when our bodies are young and healthy, but as we begin to age or get sick, we have few reserves or energy to fight back.

•

CHANGING YOUR DIET

It is never too late to change your diet. I think too many people believe that a healthful diet is bland and tasteless, and therefore they procrastinate about making changes. Nothing could be further from the truth. Healthful foods are delicious and as varied as the plant kingdom. Take a close look at your diet. You probably eat the same foods over and over: hamburgers, meatloaf, chicken, eggs, doughnuts, snack cakes, and packaged cookies. Is this interesting? If you are a typical American, you eat salad twice a week! You also stop by the fast-food restaurant several times a week. This is not too exciting. But when you open your mind and your kitchen to a wide array of vegetables and fruits, grains and legumes, you can vary your diet wildly while improving your health. What could be better?

As I travel across the country lecturing on the benefits of healthful eating in general and whole-grain breads in particular, I am often approached by people who complain they simply don't have the time or resources to change their habits. "But George," they say, "I would like to have a toned, healthy body, but I just don't have time." Or, "George, fresh vegetables and whole-grain breads are more expensive than canned vegetables and white bread." Or, "George, I know a bread machine would help me eat more healthfully, but I can't afford one."

To these complaints I respond that anyone can find the time or money if *he or she really wants to*. Yes, exercise takes a chunk out of your day, but perhaps you could fit in a half hour instead of watching television, or get up 30 minutes earlier and take a brisk morning walk. If you want to, you can find time. And, yes, fresh produce may be slightly more expensive than canned, especially if it is organically grown. Yes, a bread machine is a major cash investment. But if you value your long-term health, you will find the money for good-for-you foods. Do you own a television set? A bread machine is less costly than that second TV or a VCR.

In my opinion, it all comes down to the fact that *you* are in control. You make buying decisions based on what *you* want (or need) the most. This carries into how we shop for groceries. We all eat pretty much what we want to eat, which makes it in our personal domain to change the way we eat. No one is forcing us to buy Twinkies or caffeinated soda. No one is piling our supper plates with hamburgers and fried foods. We are in charge. And we can change. We all do what we want to do most.

The best way to begin improving your diet is to make whole-grain, fresh breads part of every meal. This is easy with a bread machine, since it is no trouble at all to bake fresh bread two, three, four, or more times a week. Once the bread is made, it is a logical step to make sandwiches. And here's a point you may have missed: good-tasting, robust breads add immeasurably to the overall flavor and nutritional value of the sandwich.

Sandwiches are not unhealthful, fattening foods. Just as it's the butter and sour cream loaded onto baked potatoes that have given the tubers a bad name, it's the type of filling that goes between the bread that mars the sandwich. As I have said, I fill sandwiches with healthful, low-fat foods that never stint on flavor. I also offer recipes for soups that taste delicious served with accompanying sandwiches or thick slices of bread. I have an entire chapter devoted to spreads and condiments, so you can jazz up any sandwich with Dill-Herb Spread, Spicy Homemade Catsup, or Homemade Salsa, to name a few. I have recipes for desserts and sweet snacks to satisfy the biggest craving. And I have recipes for healthful breads that can be made in the bread machine, easily and efficiently.

BEYOND LUNCH

One of the wonderful things about owning a bread machine and making fresh bread all week long is that sandwiches and dishes that naturally go with bread move beyond the realm of lunch very quickly. The bread tastes so good, the sandwiches are so satisfying, and the soups so filling that you will be tempted to serve them for supper. And why not? Add a big green salad and the meal is complete. Many make good breakfast and brunch dishes, too, and others are perfect mid-morning, after-school, or teatime snacks. Try sandwiches as a light meal late at night, too.

I hope you will use this book over and over, and that your bread machine will chug away on your countertop four or five times a week. I hope you will try my sandwiches and then, based on what you have learned from my style of wholesome eating, will invent your own healthful sandwiches. If you already are eating a low-fat, nutritious diet, the recipes here will expand your current repertoire in delicious and valuable ways. If you are just beginning to alter your diet and your way of thinking about food, you have come to the right place. Very soon you will feel and look better—and healthful, nutritious breads will be an integral part of your life.

CHAPTER
—·—1—··—

The Healthy
Bread Kitchen

Because I am so crazy about fresh homemade bread and all the wonderful ways it serves as the foundation for so many meals, my kitchen is organized around bread baking and healthful eating. Walk into Christy's and my Montana country kitchen and there are a few things you definitely will *not* see. You will not see shelves loaded with processed, packaged foods. You will not see plastic-wrapped loaves of soft, white supermarket bread. You will not see "family-size" jars of catsup, mayonnaise, sweetened peanut butter, and grape jelly. The refrigerator will not reveal stashes of processed cheese or lunch meats. The freezer holds no frozen TV dinners, ice cream bars, or frozen hamburger patties and hot dogs. In other words, ours is *not* a typical American kitchen. Thank goodness!

What you will see when you visit our kitchen are bowls of fresh fruit, cupboards stocked with herbs and spices, whole-grain flours, sugar-free preserves, organic honey, and dried fruits. The refrigerator boasts fresh vegetables, low-fat cheeses, liquid egg substitute, and nonfat and low-fat plain yogurt. As a rule, we make our own breads, snacks, and spreads. We even make our own catsup, mustard, and mayonnaise (made with liquid egg substitute).

I prefer to eat and cook with whole foods that are as close to their natural state as possible, but this does not mean I believe in cooking as my grandparents did. I support wholeheartedly the modern conveniences. If I did not, I would not be a bread-machine advocate—some say a fanatic!

The bread machine makes it possible, practical, and logical to have fresh-baked bread all the time. Let's face it: without this particular piece of modern technology, few of us would be able to make this claim, since life rarely affords the time necessary to make bread by hand.

I admire the dedication of my ancestors to bread baking. My great-grandmother took great pride in the bread she baked weekly to keep her family nourished. My great-grandfather planted, tended, and harvested the yearly wheat crops and ground the grains into flour so that it would always be possible to bake the life-giving bread. There was nothing arbitrary about the process. It meant survival. My grandmother taught my mother to bake bread, just as her mother had taught her, and her mother, her. My mother taught her nine children the art of baking bread, and because as a family we believed in eating whole-grain breads, early on I mastered the task of baking hearty, wholesome loaves, the sort I prefer to this day. I made loaves by hand for years; I even owned my own bakery. And then I discovered the bread machine for home use and it changed my life.

•

HOW THE BREAD MACHINE CHANGES YOUR LIFE

This handy kitchen appliance can change your life because, once you bring it home, you are able to produce fresh, nutritious bread everyday. You can put the ingredients in the canister and program the machine so that the bread is ready when you are, whether that is in a few hours, late in the afternoon after work, or the next morning after a good night's rest.

The best part of investing in a bread machine is that you can scratch "bread" right off the shopping list. In its place goes such good-sounding (and low-cost) ingredients as whole wheat flour, honey, and yeast. I say this is the best part, not because buying bread from the supermarket is expensive or difficult, but because I believe most commercial loaves are nutritionally bankrupt. Read the labels. The flour listed is most likely wheat flour, which means it is white flour. To be the least bit nutritious, this flour must be enriched with four of the twenty-six essential nutrients stripped from it during milling! Does this make sense? Only if the flour listed on the label is whole wheat will you be getting valuable nutrients. But with a bread machine you don't have to worry about labels. You control exactly what ingredients go into the bread, and hence which vitamins and minerals nourish your family. And never again will you have to eat three- or four-day-old bread. Fresh bread will become a household staple.

When you bake bread following my recipes for the appropriate size machine, the finished loaves emerge from the baking canister beautifully browned and nicely rounded every time. Such consistency is worth a lot. The machine eliminates guesswork. You never have to wonder if you let the bread rise too much or not enough, or baked it for the right amount of time or overbaked it. The machine does it all.

If you have baked bread in a conventional oven during the height of the summer, you know how hot the kitchen can get. With the bread machine, you don't have to preheat the oven, stand in front of an open oven door to check the bread for doneness, or let the large oven cool down. The self-contained bread machine mixes, kneads, rises, *and* bakes the bread. Then it turns itself off. It doesn't heat up the kitchen, although it allows the heady aroma of baking bread to escape. Finally, the bread machine requires only 120 volts of power, while most electric ovens need 240 volts. Without preheating time and with its automatic shut-off, the machine protects your electric bill (or your natural gas bill if you have a gas oven).

Baking bread in a machine is mess- and fuss-proof, too. There are no mixing bowls or sticky bread pans to wash and put away. The baking canister requires only a quick rinse and toweling off before it is stowed in the machine for the next time.

·

HOW THE BREAD MACHINE WORKS

The electric bread machine duplicates the four essential steps required for bread baking: mixing, kneading, rising, and baking. All four are performed in the same container, and not one requires human intervention. If you like, you can choose the dough cycle and remove the risen dough to make free-form loaves and rolls.

The bread machine sits easily on the countertop, taking up about as much room as a food processor. Inside, a rectangular bread canister, or bread case, fits over a kneading drive shaft onto which is secured a removable kneading blade. When the recipe ingredients are put in the canister and the machine is switched on, this blade first stirs the ingredients and then, with a shift of action, kneads the dough for a programmed period of time. After the dough is kneaded, it rises inside the gently warmed bread canister. If you peek through the viewing window at the end of the rising time, you will see that the soft dough has risen nearly to the rim of the bread case. At this point the bread machine automatically raises its internal temperature and the bread bakes. When done, the machine beeps. Does this sound easy? You bet it is.

The bread recipes on pages 180 through 235 were developed for the Breadman bread machine, and consequently may need minor adjustments for other electric bread machines. My machine is specially equipped to mix and knead robust whole-grain flours, a feature I particularly appreciate and that is clearly indicated on the control panel. The Breadman provides a Basic Wheat setting with three options: light, medium, and dark. The recipes direct you to the appropriate setting. The chart on pages 14 through 17 explains the various settings on most other electric bread machines on the market. The chart also instructs you how to adjust the recipes for the different machines.

Depending on the setting required for a recipe, the Breadman can take from two hours and twenty minutes to three hours and forty minutes to bake a loaf of bread. To help you get to know the machine before you use it, I have listed the times of the various cycles on page 12. These times apply only to the Breadman, although other machines may have similarly timed cycles.

When you buy a bread machine, read the manual carefully. Operating instructions are similar but not identical, and no two machines perform exactly alike. I believe my machine produces the best-tasting breads with the most pleasing textures. It is fitted with a 60 inch long power cord so that the machine can be positioned at a convenient distance from the nearest socket. The timer spans two-and-a-half hours to twelve hours and five minutes. If the thermal

TO BAKE A LOAF OF BREAD IN THE BREADMAN

These times represent the total time required for the entire bread-making process, including mixing, kneading, rising, and baking. At the end of baking, the machine beeps three times and turns itself off.

Basic Wheat, Light setting:	2 hours, 20 minutes
Basic Wheat, Medium setting:	2 hours, 30 minutes
Basic Wheat, Dark setting:	2 hours, 35 minutes
Fruit and Nut setting:	3 hours, 40 minutes
European setting:	3 hours, 40 minutes

TO MAKE DOUGH IN THE BREADMAN

This time represents the total time required for the dough-making process, including mixing, kneading, and rising. At the end of the cycle, the machine beeps.

Dough setting:	1 hour, 20 minutes

TO KNEAD THE DOUGH

The machine beeps partway through each kneading cycle to indicate it is time to add ingredients such as nuts or raisins, if appropriate for the recipe. If no additional ingredients are called for in the recipe, ignore the beep.

Basic Wheat setting:	20-minute kneading cycle; machine beeps 12 minutes into cycle
Fruit and Nut setting:	20-minute kneading cycle; machine beeps 12 minutes into cycle
European setting:	15-minute kneading cycle; machine beeps 7 minutes into cycle

temperature of the baking cavity reaches 370° F., the Breadman automatically turns off, regardless of whether the bread is done. This safety feature is designed to make you feel secure about leaving the appliance plugged in when you are away from the house.

•

CARING FOR THE BREAD MACHINE

Because there is only one moving part in the bread machine, care and maintenance are simple. The kneading blade rotates on its shaft and is easily removed for cleaning with a damp sponge or cloth. If it sticks, pour a little warm water into the bread case to help loosen it. Use wooden toothpicks to clean the hole for the kneading shaft, should it get clogged with dough.

The bread case, fashioned from nonstick metal, needs only a sponging with mild soap and water inside and out. Never leave the case submerged in water, and treat the nonstick coating gently—no steel-wool pads or metal implements! Clean the outside casing and the inside of the baking cavity with a damp cloth, taking care to wipe away any stray crumbs.

Never attempt to clean the bread machine unless it is unplugged and completely cool. Store the machine after wiping it clean and making certain it is dry.

•

OTHER ESSENTIALS FOR A HEALTHY BREAD KITCHEN

I also believe that every health-conscious cook should outfit his or her kitchen with a food processor, blender, and toaster oven, as well as with a bread ma-

ADJUSTMENTS FOR USING OTHER BREAD MACHINES PLUS SETTING AND CYCLE INFORMATION

BREAD MACHINE	BASIC WHEAT SETTING	EUROPEAN SETTING	FRUIT & NUT SETTING	DOUGH SETTING	SPECIAL ADJUSTMENTS, IF ANY
Breadman 1 pound & 1½ pounds	Basic Wheat setting	European setting	Fruit & Nut setting	Dough setting	None
Chefmate HB-12W	Standard setting	French Bread setting	Sweet setting	Dough setting	None
Dak	White Bread setting	French Bread setting	Sweet setting	Manual setting	For all recipes, add 2 tablespoons (1 ounce) water & ½ teaspoon yeast
Hitachi HB-B101/ B201 1½ pounds	Bread setting	Bread setting	Mix Bread setting	Knead setting	For all Elite recipes, add ½ teaspoon yeast

	White Bread setting	French Bread setting	Sweet Bread setting	Manual setting	For all recipes, add 2 tablespoons (1 ounce) water & ½ teaspoon yeast
Magic Mill Auto Bakery 101 1½ pounds	White Bread setting	French Bread setting	Sweet Bread setting	Manual setting	
300 1 pound	Auto setting	Auto setting	Auto setting	Manual setting	None
Maxim Accu-Bakery BB-1 1 pound	Standard setting	French Bread setting	Rye Bread setting	Dough setting	None
MK Seiko Home Bakery					
HB-12W 1 pound	Standard setting	French Bread setting	Sweet setting	Dough setting	None
Mister Loaf HB-210/215 1½ pounds	Standard setting	French Bread setting	Sweet setting	Dough setting	None

BREAD MACHINE	BASIC WHEAT SETTING	EUROPEAN SETTING	FRUIT & NUT SETTING	DOUGH SETTING	SPECIAL ADJUSTMENTS, IF ANY
National/Panasonic					
SD-B155P 1 pound	Basic Bake setting	Basic Bake setting	Basic Bake setting	Dough setting	None
SD-BT10P 1 pound	Basic Bake setting	Basic Bake setting	Basic Bake setting	Dough setting	None
SD-BT65N 1½ pounds	Basic Bake setting	Crisp setting	Basic Bake setting	Dough setting	For all recipes, decrease yeast by ½ teaspoon and add 2 tablespoons (1 ounce) water
Regal K6772	Bread setting	Bread setting	Raisin Bread setting	Dough setting	None
Sanyo	Bread setting	Basic White setting	Bread setting	Dough setting	None

Welbilt

ABM-100 1½ pound	White Bread setting	French Bread setting	Sweet setting	Manual setting	For all recipes, add 2 tablespoons water (1 ounce) and ½ teaspoon yeast
ABM 300/ 350/600 1 pound	Auto setting	Auto setting	Auto setting	Manual setting	None
Zojirushi BBCC-S15 1½ pounds	Basic White setting	French Bread setting	Raisin Bread setting	Dough setting	For all recipes, add 2 tablespoons (1 ounce) water and ½ teaspoon yeast

chine. I call for using these appliances in a number of the recipes, although you can make most of them without fancy equipment.

It's also nice to have a hand-held electric mixer, an electric rice cooker, a hand-cranked pasta machine, an air popcorn popper, a juice extractor, a crock pot, and an electric or hand-cranked grain grinder. None of these is called for in any recipe, but I find them handy in the kitchen.

When it comes to utensils, the most important for bread baking are a generous cutting board and a good bread knife. If you plan to make bread by hand, have ceramic or glass mixing bowls in different sizes. It's also important to have dry and liquid measures—dry measures being of graduated sizes so that you can sweep the dry ingredients equal with the rim of the measuring cup. Have at least one set of measuring spoons, and if you can find any with long handles, grab them—they are great for dipping into flour sacks. I also recommend a good supply of wooden spoons, rubber spatulas and scrapers, and at least one pair of tongs.

Stock your kitchen with heavy baking sheets (sometimes called cookie sheets), a cake pan that measures approximately 9 by 13 inches, muffin tins, and bread pans of all sizes, but especially one or two that measure 8½ by 4½ by 2¾ inches, or a 9- by 5-inch will work. Don't neglect sturdy wire cooling racks and a good colander.

You will also need a rolling pin, garlic press, wire whisks, graters and zesters, and basting brushes. Add to this list practical items such as cheesecloth, plastic wrap, kitchen towels, aprons, and potholders and your kitchen is just about complete.

CHAPTER
—·—2—·—

Why I Believe in
Whole Grains and Other
Wholesome Foods

To me, processed foods are just that: processed. Some processing is necessary to make foods digestible, palatable, or both, but too much processing can strip foods of vital nutrients, rendering them mere shadows of their former wholesome selves. Take the example of all-purpose flour, the flour everyone carries home from the supermarket in five-pound sacks. I consider it grossly nutritionally deficient.

This flour begins as life-giving wheat, but once the grain reaches the mill for grinding into flour, it is processed to such a degree that the healthful bran and germ are removed and only the starchy endosperm remains. The endosperm is then ground into the fine white powder we familiarly call "flour." The bran and germ are discarded—and with them twenty-six nutrients. Modern food technology compensates for this loss of nutrients by replacing four of the twenty-six—namely, niacin, iron, thiamin, and riboflavin (part of the B complex). And then they have the audacity to call this flour "enriched"!

Long ago, when most flour was ground from whole grains, pure white flour was considered very fancy. As milling technology improved, so did the availability of "white" flour. In the South, this was the flour of choice for tender biscuits and light, sweet cakes. It became a status symbol to bake with white flour, and only those too poor to afford it still used whole-grain flour. Happily, the tables have turned and whole-grain flour, particularly whole wheat flour, is easy to find and widely used.

Nevertheless, for the giant food companies that market it, white flour is still more practical than whole-grain flour. Because the heavy bran and oily germ are removed, the flour has an extended shelf life. The oils in the germ cause whole-grain flour to turn rancid in a few months, although the home baker can extend its shelf life a little by keeping it in the freezer. I think it's a good idea to let the flour return to room temperature before using it. Also, never buy more flour than you will realistically need in a month of baking. With the bread machine in constant use, this could be quite a lot!

•

A DESCRIPTION OF FLOUR

All grains are composed of three parts: bran, endosperm, and germ (or embryo). The bran is the tough outer layer and the germ is the center. The endosperm lies beneath the bran and surrounds the germ and is composed primarily of starch. In wheat, the endosperm contains the gluten protein that is vital to bread baking. Not all grains have gluten, which explains why most bread recipes call for a percentage of wheat flour to help raise the loaf. (For more on gluten, see page 239.)

Whole-grain flour is ground from the whole grain and contains the bran, germ, and endosperm. The bran provides good fiber, while the germ supplies the most essential oils, vitamins, and minerals. Wheat is the only grain that is processed into all-purpose flour because its endosperm has so much gluten it performs a myriad of baking functions. When you buy rye, oat, spelt or barley flour, for example, you are always buying whole-grain flour.

I freely admit to using white flour on occasion. Clearly, whole wheat flour is nutritionally superior, but white flour gives a lift and tenderness to some breads that cannot be achieved without it. When I buy white flour I buy only unbleached all-purpose. Why buy bleached flour? It's been processed one step further, and with chemicals! Who needs it?

Whole wheat flour contains as much gluten as white flour but the bread will be a little heavier than those made exclusively with all-purpose white flour. In most instances, I think this weightiness makes breads better. They are heartier, earthier, and without doubt more nutritious.

·

FIBER AND COMPLEX CARBOHYDRATES

Today, health specialists from nutritionists to medical doctors recommend that 55 to 60 percent of our total daily calories come from complex carbohydrates. This means four or five servings of fruits and vegetables and five or six servings of whole grains and legumes. Using the recipes in this book will help you do this easily. Many of the sandwiches and soups contain vegetables and fruit, and the breads are rich sources of fiber and complex carbohydrates.

Fiber is an essential element that cannot be digested but which passes through the body for very specific reasons. Some fiber helps reduce blood cholesterol, especially LDL ("bad" cholesterol) levels. Other fiber cleans the digestive tract and keeps it operating efficiently and effectively.

Fiber is either soluble or insoluble. Both kinds occur naturally in a wide array of foods and both are important. Soluble fiber, the kind that can dissolve in water, includes pectins, gums (such as guar gum), and mucilages. Insoluble fiber is found in cellulose, hemicellulose, and lignon. As a general rule, the fleshy part of foods contains soluble fiber, and the outer layers—skins, peels, husks—contain insoluble fiber.

Good sources of soluble fiber include oat, wheat, and rice brans, barley, oats, corn, apples, carrots, potatoes, beans, and broccoli. Good sources of insoluble fiber include legumes such as kidney and navy beans, strawberries and blackberries, pears, lima beans, and, last but not least, whole-grain breads.

The health benefits of a high-fiber diet are many. When you consume a high-fiber, high-complex-carbohydrate diet you will never be constipated, you will naturally lose weight and then maintain your new weight, your blood cholesterol will lower, and you will feel more alert during the day and sleep better at night because your body is utilizing its energy efficiently.

Evidence points to other benefits, too. With a high-fiber diet you are less likely to suffer from hemorrhoids, from irritable bowel syndrome, from diverticulosis, and, perhaps, from ulcers. It may prevent gallstones, varicose veins, and the chance of appendicitis and Crohn's disease. Because it lowers blood cholesterol, fiber helps prevent atherosclerosis, the recognized "common denominator" of cardiovascular disease, and it keeps blood sugars in good balance.

Some studies support theories that a high-fiber, high-complex-carbohydrate diet helps prevent colon, prostate, rectum, intestinal, and breast cancers. New research may link it to preventing other cancers, too. A diet high in fiber and complex carbohydrates is routinely prescribed for diabetics.

Our bodies need carbohydrates for energy. They act as fuel to keep our brains, muscles, and internal organs functioning. We do not store most of the calories from carbohydrates and therefore must replace them every day. On the other hand, we readily store calories derived from fat, which unhappily are much harder to burn than calories from carbohydrates. The latter are used up efficiently and quickly.

Sugars—glucose, fructose, and sucrose—are simple carbohydrates, and while we need these as much as the more complex carbohydrates, they are easy to come by. They are found in fruits and vegetables. We also consume simple carbohydrates when we eat refined sugars and syrups. Eating a balanced diet rich in fruits and vegetables provides the body with more than enough simple carbohydrates. There is no need to *add* sugar.

Complex carbohydrates are all those foods we used to refer to as starches. Time was when *starch* was a bad word, but we have learned better. Foods high in complex carbohydrates, which include grains and starchy vegetables, are essentially fat- and cholesterol-free. They are rich in valuable vitamins and minerals, they fill you up without adding fat-laden calories, and they are terrific sources of dietary fiber. The vitamin most associated with whole grains is the B complex, a grouping that includes thiamin (B_1), riboflavin (B_2), and niacin (B_3). The B vitamins are essential for metabolizing complex carbohydrates so that the body receives the energy it needs. They contribute to maintaining a healthy cholesterol level, protect against some cancers, and contribute significantly to healthy skin and hair. The B complex is available in legumes, green leafy vegetables, sprouts, and nutritional yeast, as well as in whole grains, so deficiencies are rare. Essential minerals, particularly calcium, iron, and zinc, also occur naturally in many whole grains and whole-grain flours.

•

THE BEST WAY TO EAT A HEALTHY DIET

In my last book, I talked about the 70/30 rule. I believe in this wholeheartedly. What it means is that approximately 70 percent of the time you should make a determined effort to eat as healthfully as you possibly can. Make whole-grain breads, organic produce, legumes, and fresh juices the focus of your daily diet. Forgo refined sugar, bleached all-purpose flour, animal fats, dairy products, and meats. But the rest of the time, *try* to eat healthfully but do not panic if you fail. The accompanying stress is as dangerous to your health as a dozen glazed doughnuts.

The key to maintaining a healthful diet and lifestyle is balance in all things. Eat sensibly, exercise regularly, and don't splurge too often. When you find balance, you will eat better, be healthier, feel less stress, and find time for the activities that mean the most.

The recipes in this book reflect the 70/30 philosophy. While none of the sandwich, soup, or spread recipes calls for red meat or heavy cream, there are occasions when I use whole-milk cheddar cheese, turkey bacon, or poached chicken. Most of the time, I eat a vegetarian diet but I am not so strict that I never allow myself a change of menu every now and again. I also understand that many readers may want to eat a healthful diet but are reluctant to give up poultry, fish, and dairy products.

I urge those people to buy organic, range-fed chickens and turkeys, if possible. These may be more expensive and harder to find than supermarket poultry, but most natural foods stores and many groceries carry them or can order them. And not only are they free of growth hormones and unnecessary fat, their flavor is remarkably improved. Believe me.

It's equally important to buy fish as fresh as can be. Check for glistening skin, bright eyes (if the fish is whole), and a clean, oceanlike smell. Nothing fishy!

In a number of the sandwiches and soups, I call for ground turkey, turkey ham, turkey sausage, and, on occasion, turkey franks. These products are undeniably better for you than their beef and pork versions, but they should be consumed in thoughtful moderation. I cannot deny that turkey ham and turkey franks represent processed foods; I include them to satisfy flavor cravings. True, these products have about half the calories and fat (or even less) of their counterparts, but some also have nitrates and other preservatives. Nitrate–and preservative–free turkey products can be found in your natural foods store freezer.

Dairy products are tough for some people to digest. About 15 percent of the population is lactose intolerant, which means these people have a lactase deficiency. Lactase is the enzyme that digests the milk sugar, lactose. Dairy products, particularly those from cows, leave these folks feeling queasy and crampy. I have a included number of dairy-free breads (page 220).

In all the recipes calling for yogurt, you can use either low-fat or nonfat yogurt. It makes no difference. (Except you do get a thicker spread from low-fat yogurt.) If possible, buy yogurt containing acidophilus bacteria or make sure the package label says it contains "active cultures." Both promote antibacterial activity. Another benefit of yogurt is that many people who have trouble digesting other dairy products can tolerate yogurt, which is an excellent source of calcium as well as a powerful bacteria fighter.

When it comes to mayonnaise, I hope you will make your own. I have developed a recipe for Homemade Yolk-Free Mayonnaise (page 111), made with liquid egg substitute, that is spectacular—and easy. Making mayonnaise at home with whole eggs presents a couple of problems that my recipe eliminates: there is no danger of salmonella contamination and the mayonnaise is cholesterol-free because I use liquid egg substitute. However, inevitably there will be times when you must turn to commercial mayonnaise. When you do, I recommend those labeled "reduced-calorie" or "low-fat" rather than those labeled "cholesterol-free." The former are less processed than the latter, and therefore are better for you. All commercial mayonnaises are made from pasteurized eggs and represent no danger from salmonella bacteria. When using mayonnaise at all, do so in small amounts. Two tablespoons easily is enough for two sandwiches.

•

THE BENEFITS OF EATING WELL

Overall, people who reject a high-fat, protein-heavy diet and replace it with a high-fiber, high-carbohydrate one soon feel better and, without trying, often lose weight. They are also able to maintain their weight without trouble. This style of eating does away with the concept of "dieting." Instead, we are eating healthfully and well—and relishing every mouthful without feeling guilty.

Turn to the recipes in this book. I have dozens upon dozens of healthful sandwiches, lots of nourishing soups and stews, and a fair share of satisfying desserts. And, of course, I have the breads. All are tasty, wholesome, and tailor-made for the bread machine. Once you begin incorporating these into your daily life, you will be well on the way to a lifetime of healthful eating.

CHAPTER
—·—3—·—

Traditional Sandwiches Made Healthy

As you glance at the recipe titles in this chapter you will notice lots of terms with a familiar ring: chicken salad, tuna salad, peanut butter, sardines, turkey club. Yes, you've *heard* them before but you have yet to taste *my* versions of these American favorites. If you liked these sandwiches the way Mom made them, you'll *love* them the way I make them!

First, as are all the sandwiches in the book, they are made with fresh-baked homemade bread. This fact alone places these creations head and shoulders above the ordinary. And the bread machine makes it all possible. Second, I have modified classic recipes and combinations so that they are deliciously healthful. Of the more obvious alterations, for instance, is my Crab Louis Sandwich. Traditional Crab Louis is served with a dressing made with heavy cream. That ingredient went out the window right off. My dressing is made with a little yolk-free mayonnaise and homemade catsup—and it tastes just right. On a more subtle level, I make a big, satisfying club sandwich using turkey bacon (about half the fat of pork bacon).

These two examples reflect my overall philosophy as well as my more targeted thinking concerning these traditional sandwiches. I keep what is good of the old and discard what is harmful or unnecessary. As a nation of sandwich eaters, we could not imagine giving up chicken salad, tuna, bagels and cream cheese, or turkey sandwiches. And there is no reason to do so, as you will discover in the following recipes.

CLASSIC CHICKEN SALAD ON CHEDDAR CHEESE AND CHIVE BREAD

Serves 2

Few sandwich fillings are as pleasing or as popular as chicken salad. When you take the time to poach the chicken breasts yourself (and it really requires very little time), the salad is better than ever, plus there is no chance of added salt as there often is with canned chicken. I really like the way this tastes on flavorful cheddar cheese bread.

1 cup diced **Poached Chicken Breast** (page 137)
6 tablespoons **Dill-Herb Spread** (page 119)
¼ cup **chopped celery**
1 **chopped scallion**
1 tablespoon **chopped fresh parsley**
Fine sea salt
Freshly ground pepper
4 slices **Cheddar Cheese and Chive Bread** (page 190), toasted
Lettuce leaves

In a small bowl, mix the chicken with 4 tablespoons of the Dill Herb Spread, the celery, scallions, and parsley. Season to taste with salt and pepper.

Spread the remaining 2 tablespoons of Dill-Herb Spread on the bread slices. Spread the chicken salad evenly on 2 slices of bread. Top each sandwich with lettuce leaves and then with the remaining slices of bread, spread side down. Cut into halves and serve.

TURKEY BACON, GREENS, AND TOMATO ON MULTIGRAIN BREAD

Serves 2

In some circles, BLTs are almost as traditionally American as PBJs. But why use fatty, high-calorie pork bacon when turkey rashers are leaner? Each slice contains about thirty calories as compared to nearly fifty for pork bacon, and the fat content is half that of pork. This is not to claim that turkey bacon is health food; it is not. But a little goes a long way in terms of taste and when paired with a luscious, ripe tomato, your favorite green and robust Multigrain Bread, it makes a sandwich that's hard to beat.

4 slices turkey bacon
2 tablespoons reduced-calorie mayonnaise
4 slices Multigrain Bread (page 201), toasted
1 large tomato, sliced
3 to 4 leaves greens, such as Boston lettuce, bibb lettuce, leaf lettuce,
    radicchio, or watercress

In a large skillet, cook the bacon over medium heat for about 8 minutes until lightly browned, turning once. Drain on paper towels. Cut each slice in half crosswise.

Spread mayonnaise on the toasted bread. Arrange 4 pieces of turkey bacon each on 2 slices of bread. Follow with tomato slices and greens. Top with the remaining bread, cut into halves, and serve.

DOUBLE TURKEY CLUB SANDWICH ON OLD-FASHIONED WHEAT BREAD

Serves 2

When the mood is on for a he-man–type sandwich, try this club. It's similar to the sort served in cafes and diners across the nation, but with a few noticeable (and important!) differences. First, it's served on nutritious wheat toast rather than the usual toasted store-bought white bread. Second, it calls for turkey bacon, which as mentioned, has about half the fat as pork bacon. And third, the bread is spread with tangy cranberry mayonnaise, made with all-fruit, sugar-free cranberry sauce. The cranberry sauce is sold in natural foods stores.

4 slices turkey bacon
2 tablespoons all-fruit natural cranberry sauce
2 tablespoons reduced-calorie mayonnaise
6 slices Old-Fashioned Wheat Bread (page 181), toasted
8 slices Roasted Turkey Breast (about 6 ounces total) (page 133)
Lettuce leaves or watercress sprigs, rinsed and patted dry

In a large skillet, cook the bacon over medium heat for about 6 to 8 minutes until lightly browned, turning once. Drain on paper towels. Cut each slice in half crosswise.

In a small bowl, combine the cranberry sauce and mayonnaise. Spread a third of the cranberry mayonnaise on 2 slices of the toasted bread. Arrange the turkey slices on each and then top each with another slice of bread. Spread these slices with half the remaining mayonnaise and arrange the lettuce and turkey bacon on top. Spread the rest of the mayonnaise on the last 2 slices of bread and place them, mayonnaise side down, on top of the bacon. Secure each sandwich with 2 toothpicks, cut into halves, and serve.

ALMOND-CURRY TURKEY SALAD SANDWICH ON MULTIGRAIN BREAD
Serves 6

Making turkey salad is a sensible way to use up leftover turkey, but why be sensible? Why not roast a turkey breast (as described on page 133) expressly to make this moist, highly seasoned, low-fat salad (the rest of the breast makes terrific leftovers)? If you prefer, substitute chicken or canned tuna for the turkey.

⅓ cup sliced almonds
2 tablespoons reduced-calorie mayonnaise
2 tablespoons plain nonfat yogurt
1 to 2 teaspoons curry powder
2 teaspoons fresh lemon juice
2 cups cubed turkey breast, diced into ¾-inch cubes
1 medium Granny Smith apple, peeled and finely chopped
Fine sea salt
12 slices Multigrain Bread (page 201)
1 bunch watercress, well rinsed and dried

Preheat the oven to 350°F. Spread the sliced almonds on a baking sheet and toast in the oven for about 10 minutes or until lightly browned. Stir them once or twice during toasting. Remove from oven, transfer to another baking sheet to halt cooking, and cool.

In a medium bowl, combine the mayonnaise, yogurt, curry powder, and lemon juice and mix thoroughly. Add the turkey, apple, and almonds and toss well to coat with the curry mixture. Add salt to taste.

Spread about ½ cup of the turkey salad on each of 6 slices of bread. Top each with watercress and cover with the remaining slices of bread. Cut into halves and serve.

SMOKED TURKEY WITH PEARS AND APPLE MUSTARD ON RUSSIAN BLACK BREAD
Serves 2

The heady mixture of apple butter and mustard is the perfect complement to smoked turkey and a sweet, ripe pear. When served on earthy black bread, the sandwich is just right for a cold winter's day. If you don't have time to smoke a turkey breast, buy nitrate-free delicatessen-style smoked turkey.

2 tablespoons sugar-free apple butter
2 tablespoons Dijon mustard
4 slices Russian Black Bread (page 217)
6 ounces sliced Hickory and Apple Smoked Turkey (page 135)
1 ripe pear, cored and thinly sliced

continued

In a small bowl, thoroughly combine the apple butter and mustard. Spread all 4 slices of bread with the apple-mustard mixture.

Arrange slices of turkey and pear on 2 slices of bread. Top with the remaining 2 slices of bread, apple-mustard side down. Cut into halves and serve.

TURKEY HAM SALAD SANDWICH ON OLD-FASHIONED WHEAT BREAD
Serves 2

I often rely on tangy Lemon-Mustard Spread to jazz up a simple sandwich filling, this time one that calls for turkey ham. This is fully cooked turkey that has been cured similarly to pork ham, with much of the same smoky flavor but not the same proportion of fat. It's sold in supermarkets but if you live near a good delicatessen, ask for thick-sliced turkey ham, about ½ to ¾ inch thick. As I made sandwich after sandwich for this book I realized that a tablespoon of moist spread divided between two slices of bread was adequate with most fillings. Slathering high-fat spreads on bread is one sure way to rapidly accumulate fat and calories!

1½ cups cubed cooked turkey ham (about 7½ ounces total)
¼ cup chopped celery
¼ cup chopped onion
2 tablespoons finely chopped dill pickle
6 tablespoons Lemon-Mustard Spread (page 121)
4 slices Old-Fashioned Wheat Bread (page 181)
Lettuce leaves

In a food processor, pulse the turkey ham, celery, onion, pickle, and 4 tablespoons of Lemon-Mustard Spread until very finely chopped and of spreading consistency.

Spread all 4 slices of bread evenly with the remaining Lemon-Mustard Spread. Spread the turkey ham salad equally on 2 slices and top with lettuce. Top with the remaining 2 slices of bread, spread side down. Cut into halves and serve.

PEANUT BUTTER–APPLE SANDWICH ON 100 PERCENT WHOLE WHEAT BREAD

Serves 2

Pairing dried apples with peanut butter makes a satisfying, sweet sandwich that is filling and nutritious. Think of it as a healthy peanut butter and jelly sandwich. Kids love these; pack them in lunch boxes when you want to make sure yours get a stick-to-your-ribs lunch that won't end up in the school cafeteria trash barrel. Substitute other dried fruit for the apples, such as dates, figs, apricots, pears, and raisins. All are good and all are easily available. Look for unsulfured dried fruits. These have not been treated with sulfur dioxide or potassium sorbate and some are made from pesticide-free fruit. Read the label.

¼ cup natural peanut butter
2 tablespoons honey

continued

4 slices 100 Percent Whole Wheat Bread (page 199)
⅓ cup chopped dried apples

In a small bowl, mix the peanut butter with the honey. Spread the sweetened peanut butter evenly on all 4 slices of bread.

Top 2 slices with dried apples, pressing gently so that the apples adhere to the bread. Top with the remaining 2 slices, spread side down. Cut into halves and serve.

TUNA SALAD ON CHEDDAR CHEESE AND CHIVE BREAD

Serves 2

This variation on a familiar theme replaces the expected mayonnaise with a tangy Lemon-Mustard Spread and a good dash of tamari. The cheese bread provides extra flavor, but certainly can be substituted with your favorite sandwich bread.

1 6-ounce can water-packed tuna
4 tablespoons Lemon-Mustard Spread (page 121)
⅓ cup chopped dill pickle
1½ teaspoons low-sodium tamari or soy sauce
1 teaspoon lemon juice

4 slices Cheddar Cheese and Chive Bread (page 190)
4 romaine lettuce leaves

Drain and flake the tuna. Mix it with the spread, chopped pickle, tamari, and lemon juice.

Spread the tuna evenly on 2 slices of bread. Top each sandwich with lettuce and then with the remaining slices of bread. Cut into halves and serve.

MARINATED TUNA SALAD ON FRENCH WHEAT HOAGIES

Serves 3

These low-fat tuna salad sandwiches are great for picnics or office lunches because they are meant to be made ahead of time. Wrapping the assembled sandwiches in plastic compresses them so that the flavor of the marinade permeates the sandwich, including the bread.

1 tablespoon red wine vinegar
3 anchovy fillets, rinsed and finely chopped
1 garlic clove, pressed
¼ teaspoon crushed hot red pepper flakes
5 tablespoons extra-virgin olive oil
2 6-ounce cans water-packed tuna, drained

continued

¼ cup finely chopped red onion
¼ cup finely chopped green bell pepper
2 tablespoons chopped fresh basil
1 tablespoon capers, rinsed and drained
3 French Wheat Hoagies (page 186) halved lengthwise
1 large tomato, thinly sliced

In a medium bowl, whisk together the vinegar, anchovies, garlic, and red pepper flakes. Gradually whisk in the oil. Add the tuna, onion, bell pepper, basil, and capers. Mix well, cover, and refrigerate for at least 1 hour or up to 8 hours.

Drain the tuna salad, reserving the juices. Dizzle the reserved juices on the cut surfaces of the hoagies. Spread the tuna salad evenly on each of the 3 hoagie bottoms. Top with tomato slices and then with the tops of the hoagies. Press the sandwiches together gently. Wrap each in plastic and let the sandwiches stand at room temperature for at least 1 hour and no longer than 4 or 5 hours before serving.

SARDINE SANDWICH ON RUSSIAN BLACK BREAD

Serves 2

For many people, sardines are as much of a cupboard staple as canned tuna. Like all oil-rich fish, they are an excellent source of omega-3 fish oil, which is credited with all sorts of health benefits. Studies indicate that omega-3 may be linked to prevention of heart disease, some cancers, migraines, arthritis, and high blood pressure. Taking in a sufficient amount of fish is easy, particularly when presented in a sandwich as good as this. I prefer the flavor of oil-packed sardines, but you may like water-packed just as well. If so, you will save on calories and grams of fat.

1 4½-ounce can oil-packed sardine fillets
4 ounces Neufchâtel cheese, softened
2 tablespoons Lemon-Mustard Spread (page 121)
4 slices Russian Black Bread (page 217)
2 large, thin slices red onion
2 tablespoons chopped fresh parsley
Freshly ground pepper

Drain the sardines in a wire mesh strainer and rinse briefly under cold running water. Pat dry with paper towels.

In a small bowl, work the cheese and Lemon-Mustard Spread together with a rubber spatula until smooth and spreadable. Spread on each of the four slices of bread.

Arrange the sardine fillets on 2 of the slices of bread. Top each with an onion slice and sprinkle with parsley and pepper to taste. Top with the remaining bread, spread side down, cut into halves and serve.

SALMON SALAD WITH CORN, TOMATOES, AND DILL ON PUMPERNICKEL BREAD

Serves 4

It's easy to poach salmon fillets, as I explain on page 139, but if you haven't time or inclination, substitute canned salmon. Either way, this sandwich is a sure winner. And salmon is a good source of omega-3 fatty acids, which studies show may help lower cholesterol.

1½ cups flaked, skinless Poached Salmon Fillets (page 139)
½ cup corn kernels, fresh or frozen and defrosted
2 ripe plum tomatoes, seeded and chopped
¾ cup Dill-Herb Spread (page 119)
Fine sea salt
Freshly ground pepper
8 slices Pumpernickel Bread (page 215)
Watercress

In a medium bowl, mix the salmon with the corn, tomatoes, and 6 tablespoons of the Dill-Herb Spread. Season to taste with salt and pepper.

Spread the remaining Dill-Herb Spread on all 8 slices of bread. Spread the salmon salad evenly on 4 of the slices, and top each with watercress and then with the remaining slices of bread, spread side down. Cut into halves and serve.

CRAB LOUIS SANDWICH ON BASIC WHITE BREAD

Serves 2

Whenever I have the opportunity to travel to the West Coast, I am impressed with the array of seafood available from Washington to Baja. Crab is especially good, and a dish called Crab Louis came out of San Francisco earlier in this century and endures today. Traditionally, the Louis sauce for the crab is made by mixing mayonnaise with whipped cream and chili sauce. I developed my own, *much* lower fat version that is terrific.

5 tablespoons Homemade Yolk-Free Mayonnaise (page 111) or reduced-calorie mayonnaise
1 tablespoon Spicy Homemade Catsup (page 129) or low-sodium honey-sweetened commercial catsup
½ teaspoon low-sodium Worcestershire sauce
1 cup (about 6 ounces) cooked, flaked crabmeat
¼ cup chopped celery
1 small scallion, chopped
1 teaspoon fresh lemon juice

continued

1 tablespoon chopped fresh parsley
¼ teaspoon Old Bay Seasoning or herb seasoning
Hot pepper sauce
4 slices Basic White Bread (page 184)
1 medium tomato, sliced
Lettuce leaves

In a medium bowl, mix 3 tablespoons of the mayonnaise with the catsup and Worcestershire sauce. Add the crabmeat, celery, scallion, lemon juice, parsley, and Old Bay Seasoning or herb seasoning and mix well. Season to taste with hot pepper sauce.

Spread all 4 slices of bread evenly with remaining mayonnaise. Spread crab salad equally on 2 slices and top with tomato and lettuce. Top with the remaining 2 slices of bread, mayonnaise side down. Cut into halves and serve.

SMOKED SALMON ON RUSSIAN BLACK BREAD WITH DILL-HERB SPREAD

Serves 3

Salmon and dill are natural partners. If possible, buy smoked salmon in a deli that understands how to slice it very thin. Barring that option, purchase it packaged at a specialty store or good supermarket.

6 slices Russian Black Bread (page 217)
3 tablespoons Dill-Herb Spread (page 119), made without garlic
3 ounces sliced smoked salmon

Spread the Dill-Herb Spread on 3 slices of bread. Arrange the smoked salmon on the slices. Top with the remaining slices. Cut into halves and serve.

SHRIMP AND TARRAGON SPREAD ON LEMON BREAD

Serves 4

It is always a good idea to buy shrimp in the shell and then peel it yourself. This ensures a degree of freshness. Once the shrimp is cooked and chopped, it's an easy matter to combine it with other ingredients to make this classy spread.

1 pound medium shrimp, in the shell
6 ounces Neufchâtel cheese, at room temperature
2 scallions, finely chopped
½ cup finely chopped celery
3 tablespoons chopped fresh parsley
1 tablespoon fresh lemon juice
½ teaspoon Worcestershire sauce
½ teaspoon dried tarragon
¼ teaspoon fine sea salt
Dash of hot pepper sauce
8 slices Lemon Bread (page 194), toasted
1 large tomato, sliced
Lettuce leaves

Bring a saucepan of lightly salted water to a boil. Drop the shrimp into the water and cook for about 3 minutes or just until the shrimp are pink and firm. Drain, rinse well under cold water, and drain again.

Peel the shrimp and use the tip of a sharp knife to remove any dark veins running down the backs of the shrimp. Coarsely chop the shrimp and put them in a bowl.

Add the cheese, scallions, celery, parsley, lemon juice, Worcestershire sauce, tarragon, salt, and hot pepper sauce to the shrimp. Use a rubber spatula to blend the ingredients thoroughly. Cover and refrigerate for at least 1 hour to give the flavors time to blend.

Spread the shrimp mixture evenly on 4 slices of toast. Top each with tomato slices and lettuce and then with the remaining slices of toast. Cut into halves and serve.

CHAPTER
—·—4—·—
Hot Sandwiches

When I first began thinking about this book I admit I thought mainly of cold sandwiches made with easy-to-acquire ingredients that, when put between two pieces of homemade bread, taste very good. I love this kind of sandwich, but as I worked on the recipes, I found myself turning more and more to fillings made from cooked food. The results are happily apparent in the recipes that follow. These are the stuff of hearty, filling meals that go far beyond the idea of a sandwich as a snack or "throwaway" meal.

America's favorite sandwich is a cooked one: the hamburger. Thousands upon thousands of these beef patties are consumed daily—but never by me. As you know, I avoid red meat at all costs, and Christy and I encourage our children to do so as well. But that does not mean we don't enjoy a good "burger" now and then—tofu burgers, salmon burgers, nut burgers, or falafel burgers.

These may sound esoteric at first, but read the recipes to discover how accessible, truly healthful, and good-tasting they are.

As I worked on this chapter, I found myself making old favorites in new ways. Take, for example, the Denver Sandwich. Here's a western omelet sandwich made with cholesterol-free liquid egg substitute—and it tastes every bit as good, perhaps better, than the original. I was equally excited about the Turkey Loaf Sandwich. As I say in the recipe note, I had heard friends comment on how much they like meatloaf sandwiches, but it wasn't until I made my own turkey loaf and tried it in a sandwich that I understood such loyalty. Let's hope that's the kind of loyalty all these will inspire.

SWEET-AND-SOUR TURKEY STIR-FRY ON OLD-FASHIONED WHEAT BREAD

Serves 4

Stir-frying is a quick and relatively fat-free method of cooking. This one is made with thin strips of turkey ham tossed with vegetables and coated with a distinctly Asian-inspired sauce.

1 teaspoon canola oil
1 small onion, peeled, halved, and cut crosswise into ¼-inch-thick half-moons
1 red bell pepper, seeded and cut into ¼-inch strips
1 celery rib, cut diagonally into ¼-inch pieces
1 tablespoon grated fresh ginger
1 garlic clove, finely chopped
4 ounces turkey ham, cut into 3-inch strips about ¼ inch wide
½ cup unsweetened pineapple juice
1 tablespoon low-sodium tamari
½ teaspoon honey
½ teaspoon cornstarch
Freshly ground pepper
8 slices Old-Fashioned Wheat Bread (page 181)
Watercress sprigs, washed and drained

In a medium nonstick skillet, heat the oil over medium-high heat. Add the onion, bell pepper, celery, ginger, and garlic and stir-fry for 1 minute. Add the turkey ham and continue stir-frying for about 2 minutes longer or until the vegetables are crisp-tender.

In a small bowl, stir together the pineapple juice, tamari, honey, and cornstarch until the cornstarch dissolves. Pour into the skillet and cook for about 15 seconds, stirring, until the sauce thickens, reduces slightly, and glazes the turkey. Remove from the heat and season to taste with pepper.

Put a few sprigs of watercress on 4 slices of bread. Top with the turkey stir-fry and the remaining slices. Serve immediately.

1990S DENVER SANDWICH ON RUSSIAN BLACK BREAD

Serves 3

This up-to-date omelet sandwich is a variation of the classic western sandwich. The difference here is that I use cholesterol-free egg substitute and turkey breakfast sausage, the latter only about 10 percent fat (pork sausage can be as much as 30 percent fat!).

continued

4 turkey breakfast sausage links (about 5 ounces total)
½ cup water
½ cup finely chopped green bell pepper
½ cup finely chopped onion
1 cup liquid egg substitute
¼ teaspoon fine sea salt
⅛ teaspoon freshly ground pepper
6 slices Russian Black Bread (page 217), toasted
¼ cup Homemade Salsa (page 117) or commercial salsa

In a nonstick skillet, bring the turkey links and the water to a boil. Cook over medium heat for about 10 minutes or until the water is evaporated and the turkey sausage is lightly browned and cooked through. Transfer the sausage to a shallow dish and rinse out the skillet. Chop the sausage into ¼-inch dice.

Spray the skillet with nonstick cooking spray. Put the green pepper and onion in the skillet, cover, and cook over medium heat for about 5 minutes or until the vegetables are softened. Transfer to the bowl. Add the egg substitute, sausage, salt, and pepper, and whisk well.

Spray the skillet once more with the nonstick cooking spray. Add the egg mixture and cook over medium heat for about 3 minutes or until the omelet sets. During cooking, lift up the cooked portion of the omelet and tilt the skillet to allow the uncooked portion to flow underneath.

Fold the omelet over on itself into thirds. Remove from heat and slice the omelet into 3 pieces. Put one piece each on 3 slices of toast and spread with salsa. Top with the remaining slices of toast and serve immediately.

MONTE CRISTO ON
BASIC WHITE BREAD

Serves 2

Toasted Monte Cristo sandwiches are usually made with ham and cheese. Mine are made with turkey and low-sodium Swiss cheese, and are absolutely delicious. To save on fat and cholesterol, I dip the bread in egg substitute and low-fat milk before cooking the sandwiches. I like them with a sweet yogurt spread, but if you prefer, serve them with mustard.

2 3-ounce slices Roast Turkey Breast (page 133) or storebought
2 ½-ounce slices low-sodium Swiss cheese
4 slices Basic White Bread (page 184)
½ cup low-fat milk (1 percent)
½ cup liquid egg substitute
⅔ cup toasted wheat germ
⅓ cup sugar-free peach preserves (optional)
⅓ cup plain nonfat yogurt (optional)

Lay 1 slice of turkey and 1 slice of cheese on each of 2 slices of bread. Top each with the remaining slices of bread.

In a shallow bowl, whisk the milk with the egg substitute. Spread the wheat germ in a shallow dish or on a plate. Dip each sandwich into this mixture and then coat it on both sides with wheat germ.

continued

Spray a large nonstick skillet with nonstick cooking spray and heat over medium heat. Cook the sandwiches in the skillet, one at a time if necessary, for about 8 minutes, turning once, or until golden brown on both sides.

While the sandwiches are cooking, combine the peach preserves and yogurt. Cut the toasted sandwiches in half and serve immediately with the peach-yogurt mixture, if desired.

TURKEY FRENCH DIP ON FRENCH WHEAT HOAGIES

Serves 4

Where's the beef? Who cares? These simple sandwiches are made from freshly roasted turkey breast and, exactly like beef French dip, each sandwich is provided with some dipping sauce. The difference is that these are so much better for you!

Roast Turkey Breast (page 133)
3 cups Chicken Stock (page 140) or low-sodium chicken broth
Fine sea salt
Freshly ground pepper
4 French Wheat Hoagies (page 186), split lengthwise

Make the turkey breast according to the recipe. Do not discard the pan drippings.

Slice the cooked breast very thin so that you have 12 to 16 slices of turkey. Set aside. Cover and refrigerate or freeze the remaining turkey breast for another use.

Put the pan with the drippings on a burner and pour the stock into it. Bring to a boil, scraping the brown bits stuck to the pan. Season to taste with salt and pepper. Lower the heat and add the sliced turkey to the pan. Cook for 1 minute.

Lift the turkey from the pan liquid and lay an even number of slices on the bottom half of each hoagie. Top each with the top half of the hoagie.

Pour the remaining liquid from the pan into 4 small bowls. Serve the sandwiches with individual bowls of dipping sauce.

SLOPPY JOES ON MULTIGRAIN BUNS

Serves 6

I like to make sloppy Joes with practically fat-free ground turkey—and then toss in a handful of toasted wheat germ for an extra boost of protein and valuble vitamin E. Kids will love this, since it's mildly seasoned and served on big, soft buns. For a little more heat, increase the chili powder a teaspoon or so. Also, be sure to read the label for the ground turkey: some brands are as much as 15 percent fat! That's as much as ground beef. Look for those that are no more than 7 percent fat.

continued

1 large onion, chopped
½ cup chopped celery
½ cup chopped green bell pepper
1 pound ground turkey
1 15-ounce can low-sodium tomato sauce
½ cup water or low-sodium tomato juice
2 tablespoons low-sodium tomato paste
2 tablespoons lemon juice
2 tablespoons cider vinegar
1 teaspoon chili powder
1 teaspoon dried oregano
¾ teaspoon fine sea salt
¼ teaspoon freshly ground pepper
½ cup toasted wheat germ
6 Multigrain Buns, split (page 232)

In a medium, nonstick skillet, cook the onion, celery, green pepper, and turkey over medium-high heat for about 5 minutes, stirring often to break up the meat until it loses its pink color.

Stir in the tomato sauce, water or juice, tomato paste, lemon juice, vinegar, chili powder, oregano, salt, and pepper. Raise the heat and bring to a simmer. Reduce the heat to low and cook for about 15 minutes, stirring often.

Add the wheat germ and cook for about 3 minutes or until the sauce thickens a little. Serve immediately spooned over the buns.

GRILLED TURKEY FRANKS
WITH BARBECUED ONIONS
ON FRENCH WHEAT HOAGIES

Serves 4

For hot dog fans, the combination of turkey franks nestled in toasted hoagies and generously smothered with tangy onions is hard to beat. Look for turkey franks without nitrates, most frequently found in the freezer compartment of health food stores. If you prefer, split the franks and broil them for seven to ten minutes, or boil them in water for about five minutes until heated through.

4 turkey franks
4 French Wheat Hoagies (page 186)
1 cup warm Barbecued Onions (page 126)

Grill the franks over medium heat on a stovetop grill or on charcoal or gas grill for 7 to 10 minutes, turning occasionally, until heated through.

Split the hoagies in half lengthwise and toast lightly. Put the franks in the toasted hoagies and top each with ¼ cup of Barbecued Onions. Serve immediately.

TURKEY LOAF SANDWICH ON MULTIGRAIN BREAD

Serves 4

Do you like meatloaf sandwiches? Many people do, and while I don't eat red meat and therefore never became a fan of the traditional sort, I decided to try a turkey loaf sandwich. Now I see what all the fuss is about. These are great! Take care to serve the turkey loaf either warm or cold from the refrigerator. Even when cooked, it's not a good idea to leave poultry at room temperature for very long. And while the recipe makes more turkey loaf than you will need for the sandwiches, serve what you won't use for the sandwiches as you would any meatloaf, or save it for *more* sandwiches tomorrow! It keeps in the refrigerator for two to three days.

Turkey Loaf

1½ pounds ground turkey
1 cup quick-cooking oats
¾ cup low-fat milk
¼ cup liquid egg substitute
4 tablespoons finely chopped onion
4 tablespoons finely chopped fresh parsley
1 teaspoon fine sea salt
1 tablespoon low-sodium soy sauce or Worcestershire sauce
½ teaspoon finely ground pepper
¼ teaspoon dried thyme
2 tablespoons low-sodium tomato paste

Sandwich

¼ cup Dill-Herb Spread (page 119)
8 slices Multigrain Bread (page 201)

To make the turkey loaf, preheat the oven to 350°F.

Using a fork or your hands, mix all the ingredients listed for the loaf in a large bowl. Press the mixture into a 9-by-5-by-3-inch loaf pan and smooth the top. Bake for about 1 hour or until the internal temperature registers 170°F. on a meat thermometer. Let the turkey loaf cool for 10 to 15 minutes before slicing.

When slightly cool, cut 4 thick slices of turkey loaf for the sandwiches. Cover and refrigerate the remaining loaf for more sandwiches or a later meal.

To make the sandwiches, spread the Dill-Herb Spread on the bread. Top 4 slices of bread with a slice of turkey loaf and then with the remaining 4 slices of bread. Cut into halves and serve.

MOM'S CABBAGE BURGERS

Serves 6

I named these full-flavored sandwiches in honor of my mother-in-law. My wife, Christy, who grew up in Nebraska, remembers filled-pastry sandwiches very similar to these that were served in the school cafeteria on Fridays—the one day in the week that the lunch line stretched out the door! Her mother, Eunice Nielsen, devised her own recipe to please her children, and Christy brought this Nielsen family favorite with her to Montana when she married me. Our boys love them as much as Christy and I do and beg for them whenever they spy cabbage in our shopping cart. Luckily, the bread machine makes mixing up a batch of Dilled Calzone Dough fast and easy. We dip the hot, baked sandwiches in Spicy Homemade Catsup.

½ medium onion, chopped
1 garlic clove, minced
12 ounces lean ground turkey
Fine sea salt
1½ teaspoons salt-free herb and spice blend
⅛ teaspoon freshly ground pepper
About 4 cups finely shredded cabbage (approximately 10 ounces or half a
    large head)
Dilled Calzone Dough (page 197)
6 tablespoons Spicy Homemade Catsup (page 129)

Preheat the oven to 400°F.

In a medium, nonstick skillet, cook the onion, garlic, and turkey over medium heat for about 5 minutes, stirring often to break up the meat until it loses its pink color.

Stir in the sea salt to taste, herb and spice blend, and pepper. Add the shredded cabbage and cook, covered, for 5 to 6 minutes, stirring occasionally, until cabbage is wilted.

Divide the dough into 6 balls, set on a lightly floured surface, cover with plastic wrap or a kitchen towel, and let rest for 10 minutes. Remove the covering and roll out each ball until it is 7 to 8 inches in diameter. Spread a round with 1 tablespoon catsup, leaving a 1-inch border around the edge. Place about half a cup of the turkey filling in the center of the round. Fold in half to make a half-moon and crimp the edges closed with a fork. Pierce the top of the pastry with the fork. Repeat with the remaining 5 rounds of dough.

Arrange the pastry rounds on an ungreased baking pan, leaving about 2 inches between each one. Bake for 15 to 20 minutes or until the pastry is golden brown. Serve immediately with more catsup.

TURKEY SAUSAGE, MUSHROOM, AND ITALIAN CHEESE CALZONES

Serves 4

Once the bread machine mixes, kneads, and lets the dough rise, forming these flavor-packed calzones is fast and easy. The filling is made with turkey sausage augmented by part-skim ricotta and mozzarella cheese.

2 links sweet or hot Italian turkey sausage (about 5 ounces total), casings removed
12 large mushrooms, thinly sliced
1 cup part-skim ricotta cheese
1 cup shredded part-skim mozzarella cheese
¼ cup freshly grated Parmesan cheese
2 tablespoons chopped fresh basil, or 1½ teaspoons dried
⅛ teaspoon crushed hot red pepper flakes
Calzone Dough (page 196)
1 tablespoon olive oil

Spray a medium nonstick skillet with nonstick cooking spray. Cook the sausage and mushrooms over medium heat for about 5 minutes, stirring with a spoon to break up lumps in the sausage until the sausage is cooked through. Transfer to a medium bowl and let cool.

When the sausage and mushrooms are cool, stir in the ricotta, mozzarella, and Parmesan cheeses, basil, and pepper flakes.

Preheat the oven to 400°F.

Divide the dough into 4 balls. Set the balls on a lightly floured surface, cover with plastic wrap or a kitchen towel, and let rest for 10 minutes. Remove the covering and roll out each ball until it is 9 inches in diameter. Spoon a quarter of the filling onto the lower half of each round, leaving a 1-inch border at the bottom. Fold in half to make a half-moon. Pinch the edges together and roll the dough to form a thick rope. Pierce the top of the calzones with the tip of a sharp knife.

Brush the calzones with the oil and arrange on a baking sheet that has been sprayed with nonstick cooking spray. Cover with plastic wrap and let rise for 15 minutes.

Bake the calzones for 15 to 20 minutes or until golden brown. Cool for 5 minutes before serving.

TURKEY, ZUCCHINI, AND BASIL BURGERS ON MULTIGRAIN BUNS

Serves 4

Ground turkey is far less fatty than ground beef and so I combine it with zucchini to give it moisture and body. The scallion, basil, and garlic provide lots of good flavor. Otherwise, this is a pretty straightforward burger, served on a homemade bun with lettuce and tomato. My sons love these!

1 medium zucchini
1 pound ground turkey
2 tablespoons chopped fresh basil, or 1½ teaspoons dried
1 scallion, finely chopped
1 garlic clove, minced
Fine sea salt
Freshly ground pepper
2 tablespoons Homemade Yolk-Free Mayonnaise (page 111) or reduced-
    calorie mayonnaise
4 Multigrain Buns (page 232), split lengthwise
1 medium tomato, sliced
Red leaf lettuce

Preheat the broiler.

Shred the zucchini and then squeeze it between your fingers to remove excess moisture.

In a medium bowl, combine the zucchini, turkey, basil, scallion, and garlic and mix thoroughly. Season with salt and pepper. Form into 4 patties. Wash your hands with soap and hot water before proceeding with the recipe.

Broil the burgers about 4 inches from the heat for about 12 minutes, turning once. Test for doneness by pressing them in the center. When done, they will feel quite firm.

Spread the buns with mayonnaise. Place the cooked burgers on the bottom halves of the buns and top with tomato slices and lettuce. Replace the top halves of the buns and serve.

TURKEY BARBECUE AND COLESLAW ON MULTIGRAIN BUNS

Serves 6

We really like the sensation of eating hot turkey with cold, creamy coleslaw. Cabbage is a valuable source of vitamin C, beta-carotene, and sulfur and as the primary ingredient in coleslaw helps to make this a healthful sandwich. Coleslaw does not have to be oily and fattening. Mine is made with only a half-cup of low-fat mayonnaise; divide that six ways and you don't have much to worry about in terms of fat.

continued

Coleslaw
½ cup Homemade Yolk-Free Mayonnaise (page 111) or reduced-calorie
    mayonnaise
¼ cup cider vinegar
1 tablespoon honey
4 cups shredded cabbage, or 8 ounces storebought coleslaw mix
1 large carrot, shredded
2 scallions, finely chopped
¼ teaspoon fine sea salt
⅛ teaspoon freshly ground pepper (optional)

Sandwich
1 pound thinly sliced Hickory and Apple Smoked Turkey (page 135) or
    deli-style smoked turkey
1 cup Homemade Barbecue Sauce (page 127)
6 Multigrain Buns (page 232), sliced lengthwise

To make the coleslaw, in a medium bowl, mix the mayonnaise, vinegar, and honey. Add the cabbage, carrot, and scallions. Mix well. Season with salt and pepper. Refrigerate until serving.

To make the sandwich, in a medium nonstick skillet, heat the turkey slices with the barbecue sauce over medium heat for about 3 minutes until heated through.

Spoon the turkey slices and sauce evenly over the bottom halves of the buns. Top each with about ¼ cup of the coleslaw and then with the top halves of the buns. Serve immediately, with the remaining coleslaw on the side.

GRILLED CHICKEN SANDWICH ON OLD-FASHIONED WHEAT BREAD
Serves 2

A warm grilled chicken sandwich is easier to make than a chicken salad sandwich, although most folks think of them as being exotic. Pound the boned breasts a little to make them cook faster, and make sure they are skinless. The skin of the poultry contributes the most fat. While I like to use a stovetop grill, you can cook chicken breasts under the broiler about 4 inches from the heat. They are done in about 5 minutes.

2 **boneless, skinless chicken breasts (about 4 ounces each)**
2 **½-ounce slices low-fat Swiss cheese**
Dill-Herb Spread (page 119)
4 **slices toasted Old-Fashioned Wheat Bread (page 181)**
4 **fresh mushrooms, thinly sliced**
Alfalfa sprouts

Using a meat pounder or a rolling pin, flatten the chicken breasts slightly between 2 sheets of plastic wrap.

Spray a stovetop grill with nonstick cooking spray and cook the breasts 3 to 4 minutes to a side or until cooked through. Lay a slice of cheese on each breast, remove them from the heat, and cover. Let stand for 1 minute or until cheese melts.

Spread the Dill-Herb Spread on each slice of bread. Put a cooked chicken breast on 2 of the slices. Top with the mushroom slices, a handful of sprouts, and the remaining slices of bread. Cut into halves and serve.

AVOCADO AND MUSTARD GRILLED CHICKEN ON MULTIGRAIN BUNS

Serves 4

I've noticed that every fast-food restaurant in the country proudly advertises a chicken fillet sandwich. The truth is, those sandwiches are made from breaded, fried chicken and are not particularly low in anything (saturated fat or calories), except perhaps flavor! Mine, made with broiled skinless chicken breasts and served with healthful avocado and tomato slices, is a sandwich to be justly proud of. You can, if you prefer, grill the chicken breasts (see Grilled Chicken Sandwich on Old-Fashioned Wheat Bread, page 65, for instructions).

4 boneless, skinless chicken breasts (about 4 ounces each)
Fine sea salt
Freshly ground pepper
¼ cup Lemon-Mustard Spread (page 121)
4 Multigrain Buns (page 232), sliced
1 medium avocado, peeled, pitted, and sliced
2 ripe medium tomatoes, sliced

Preheat the broiler.

Using a meat pounder or a rolling pin, flatten the chicken breasts slightly between 2 sheets of plastic wrap. Season the chicken to taste with salt and pepper.

Broil the chicken about 4 inches from the heat, turning once, for about 4 minutes or until lightly browned on both sides. Brush the side facing up with Lemon-Mustard Spread and broil for about 2 minutes longer or until the spread becomes a brown, bubbling glaze.

Place the chicken breasts on the bottom halves of the buns, top with avocado and tomato slices, and then the top halves of the buns. Serve immediately.

OPEN-FACED TUNA MELT ON LEMON BREAD

Serves 2

Mixing water-packed tuna with low-fat yogurt and piquant Lemon-Mustard Spread is a good way to enjoy this protein-rich fish without a lot of added fat. The Lemon Bread accentuates the Lemon-Mustard Spread, but you could substitute Old-Fashioned Wheat Bread (page 181) or another bread. The sandwich is easy to make in a toaster oven if you prefer not to turn on the broiler.

continued

1 6½-ounce can water-packed tuna, drained
2 tablespoons plain low-fat yogurt
2 tablespoons Lemon-Mustard Spread (page 121)
1 tablespoon chopped red onion
1 tablespoon fresh lemon juice
1 tablespoon snipped fresh chives, or 1 teaspoon dried
Small pinch of cayenne pepper
2 slices Lemon Bread (page 194), toasted
½ cup shredded low-fat Swiss or cheddar cheese

Preheat the broiler.

Flake the tuna into a small bowl. Add the yogurt, Lemon-Mustard Spread, onion, lemon juice, chives, and cayenne pepper and mix well.

Spread tuna on both slices of the bread and sprinkle with cheese. Broil 3 to 4 inches from the heat source for 1 to 2 minutes or until the cheese melts. Serve immediately.

SALMON BURGER ON A MULTIGRAIN BUN

Serves 3

The food processor makes quick work of chopping the salmon so that it blends easily with the vegetables and mayonnaise and the mixture can be formed into patties. They are a healthful and delicious alternative to meat patties. If you dip your hands in water first, the salmon burgers will not stick to them. I recommend fresh salmon for these burgers, but canned salmon works well, too. Use three six-ounce cans.

1 pound skinless and boneless salmon fillets (about 1¼ pounds before preparation), cut into pieces
2 tablespoons chopped celery
2 tablespoons chopped scallions
2 tablespoons chopped fresh parsley
3 tablespoons fresh whole wheat bread crumbs
3 tablespoons Homemade Yolk-Free Mayonnaise (page 111) or reduced-calorie mayonnaise
1 teaspoon salt-free herb and spice blend
½ teaspoon fine sea salt
¼ teaspoon freshly ground pepper
3 Multigrain Buns (page 232), split and toasted
6 tablespoons spicy Homemade Salsa (page 117) or commercial salsa
Red leaf lettuce

continued

In a food processor fitted with a metal blade, pulse the salmon fillets until finely chopped. Transfer to a medium bowl and add the celery, scallion, parsley, bread crumbs, mayonnaise, herb seasoning, salt, and pepper and mix thoroughly. Using wet hands, form the mixture into 3 rounds, 3½ inches each, and place on a waxed paper–lined tray until ready to cook.

Spray a large nonstick skillet with nonstick cooking spray. Cook the salmon burgers over medium-high heat for about 3 minutes, turning once, or until lightly browned on both sides. This produces medium-rare burgers; cook them a little longer for medium or well-done burgers.

Place the burgers on the bottom halves of the buns. Top each with a dollop of the salsa, some lettuce leaves, and then with the top halves of the buns. Serve immediately.

GRILLED SWORDFISH ON GARDEN O' PLENTY BREAD

Serves 2

This is a very fancy sandwich, made with grilled swordfish and piquant sun-dried tomatoes, and is one you could serve for a weekend lunch party or for supper. Or make it anytime you want a tasty treat. The homemade bread makes the meal just as special as the fish or the spread. And keep in mind how good fish is for you. Not only is it low in fat, it's high in omega-3 oil.

1 tablespoon fresh lemon juice
1 tablespoon olive oil
½ teaspoon dried oregano
1 garlic clove, crushed
Fine sea salt
Freshly ground pepper
2 5-ounce swordfish steaks, each barely ½ inch thick
4 slices Garden O' Plenty Bread (page 223), toasted
¼ cup Sun-Dried Tomato Mayonnaise (page 114)
1 medium tomato, sliced
2 tablespoons shredded fresh basil

In a shallow bowl, combine the lemon juice, oil, oregano, garlic, salt, and pepper. Add the swordfish steaks and turn them a few times to coat. Cover and refrigerate, turning occasionally, for 1 hour.

Preheat the broiler or prepare a charcoal grill.

Drain the swordfish and discard the marinade. Broil or grill the fish about 4 inches from the heat for about 4 minutes, turning once, or until lightly browned for medium-rare. Cook longer if you like them better done.

Spread all 4 slices of bread evenly with the Sun-Dried Tomato Mayonnaise. Put a swordfish steak on 2 of the slices of bread. Top each with tomato slices, basil, and then the remaining slices of bread, spread side down. Serve immediately.

ROASTED RED PEPPERS WITH GRILLED TUNA ON PUMPERNICKEL BREAD

Serves 4

Roasting red peppers magically changes the texture and flavor of this common garden vegetable. Suddenly its flavor is sweet and slightly smoky—just right for topping grilled tuna steaks.

2 red bell peppers
4 teaspoons balsamic or cider vinegar
Fine sea salt (optional)
Freshly ground pepper (optional)
4 5-ounce tuna steaks, about ½ inch thick
2 tablespoons olive oil
8 slices Pumpernickel Bread (page 215)
2 tablespoons Homemade Yolk-Free Mayonnaise (page 111) or reduced-
     calorie mayonnaise
Lettuce leaves

Position a broiler rack 4 inches from the source of heat and preheat the broiler. Broil the peppers for about 15 minutes, turning often, until charred on all sides. Put the charred peppers in a paper bag and let them cool for about 10 minutes. Using the back of a knife, scrape and peel the charred skin. Rinse the peppers under running water to remove all specks of charred skin, if you wish.

Stem, halve, and seed the peppers. Cut into ½-inch strips. Put in a bowl and toss with the balsamic vinegar and salt and pepper to taste.

Heat the broiler again or prepare a charcoal grill.

Brush the tuna on both sides with oil and season to taste with salt and pepper.

Broil or grill the tuna about 4 inches from the heat for about 4 minutes, turning once, until lightly browned for medium-rare. Cook longer if you like fish better done.

Spread 4 slices of bread with mayonnaise. Lay a tuna steak on each slice. Top with the roasted red peppers, a lettuce leaf, and the remaining slices of bread. Serve immediately.

OPEN-FACED NUT BURGER MELTS ON OLD-FASHIONED WHEAT BREAD

Serves 4

These burgers don't have a shred of meat in them, but the nuts, rice, and cheddar cheese give them body and lots of flavor. I prefer serving them on toasted bread rather than buns, and coating it with a yogurt spread for extra moistness. Make the vegetable broth with a vegetable bouillon cube sold in supermarkets and health food stores.

continued

¾ cup ground or finely chopped walnuts
1 cup shredded cheddar cheese
½ cup cooked brown rice
½ cup fresh whole wheat bread crumbs
½ cup wheat germ
½ cup liquid egg substitute
¼ cup minced onion
¼ cup vegetable stock
1 tablespoon low-sodium tamari
¼ teaspoon fine sea salt
¼ teaspoon cayenne pepper
1 garlic clove, pressed
4 thick slices tomato
¼ cup shredded part-skim mozzarella cheese
4 tablespoons Tangy Yogurt Spread (page 120)
4 slices Old-Fashioned Wheat Bread (page 181), toasted

Preheat the oven to 375°F.

Combine the nuts and cheese with the rice, bread crumbs, wheat germ, egg substitute, onion, stock, tamari, salt, cayenne, and garlic. When well mixed, shape into 4 patties and place on an ungreased nonstick baking sheet.

Bake the patties for 15 minutes. Put a tomato slice on top of each and sprinkle with 1 tablespoon of mozzarella cheese. Continue baking for about 5 minutes longer or until the cheese melts.

Spread the yogurt mixture on the toasted bread. Top each with a burger and serve.

GRILLED APPLE AND CHEDDAR CHEESE ON OATMEAL SPICE BREAD

Serves 2

Crisp apples and sharp cheddar cheese is a happy combination that tastes fabulous between two slices of toasted bread. We particularly like this version of grilled cheese sandwiches in the fall, when the Montana air is clear and cool and apples are at their peak. I suggest Granny Smith apples but any tart, firm apple will do.

4 slices Oatmeal Spice Bread (page 207)
2 tablespoons Lemon-Mustard Spread (page 121)
1 cup shredded low-sodium cheddar cheese
1 large Granny Smith apple, peeled, cored, and very thinly sliced

Preheat the broiler. Lightly toast the bread on both sides 4 to 5 inches from the heat.

Spread all 4 slices with Lemon-Mustard Spread and sprinkle each with cheese. Broil 4 to 5 inches from the heat for about 3 minutes or until the cheese melts. Arrange the apple slices on 2 slices of bread and top with the remaining bread, cheese side down. Press the tops of the sandwiches gently before cutting into halves and serving.

GRILLED CHEESE AND TOMATO ON CARAWAY RYE BREAD

Serves 2

You will note that I nearly always shred cheese and measure it by the cup. This helps avoid the temptation to lay "one more slice" of cheese on the sandwich and thus saves calories and fat. Shredded cheese melts faster, too.

4 slices Caraway Rye Bread (page 213)
2 tablespoons Dijon mustard
1 medium tomato, sliced
1 cup shredded low-fat cheddar cheese

Preheat the broiler. Lightly toast the bread on both sides 4 to 5 inches from the heat.

Spread all 4 slices with mustard. Lay tomato slices on 2 slices of bread and sprinkle these with cheese. Broil 4 to 5 inches from the heat for about 3 minutes or until the cheese melts.

Top with the remaining bread, mustard side down. Press the tops of the sandwiches gently before cutting into halves and serving.

TOFU BURGERS ON MULTIGRAIN BUNS

Serves 4

Tofu, made from soybeans, is a great vegetarian source of protein and is low in fat and sodium. The firmer the tofu, the more concentrated the vitamins and minerals, which makes these tasty burgers super healthful. Tofu cheese is a different product, although it shares many of the same nutrients and is also made from soybeans. Look for both in natural foods stores. Tofu is sold in greengrocers and supermarkets as well. Make the bread crumbs from any left-over bread, although whole wheat bread is best.

1 pound firm tofu
½ cup chopped onion
2 garlic cloves, minced
¼ cup finely chopped green or red bell pepper
½ cup fresh whole wheat bread crumbs
2 tablespoons low-sodium tamari
½ cup shredded mozzarella-style tofu cheese
1 teaspoon salt-free herb and spice blend
½ cup toasted wheat germ
4 Multigrain Buns (page 232)
4 tablespoons Guacamole (page 124)

continued

Wring the tofu in a clean kitchen towel to remove excess liquid and then mash it with a fork. Put the mashed tofu in a bowl and set aside.

Spray a nonstick skillet with nonstick cooking spray and add onion, garlic, and bell pepper. Cook over medium heat for about 5 minutes or until soft. Add the cooked vegetables, bread crumbs, tamari, tofu cheese, and herb blend to the mashed tofu and mix well.

Spread the wheat germ in a shallow dish or on a plate. Shape the tofu mixture into 4 patties about ½ inch thick. Roll each in the wheat germ, patting them so that the wheat germ adheres.

Split and lightly toast the buns, then spread with guacamole.

Spray the skillet with a little more nonstick cooking spray and heat over medium heat. Cook the tofu burgers for 2 to 3 minutes or until the undersides are lightly browned. Turn each carefully and cook the other side for another 2 to 3 minutes or until nicely browned on both sides. Place the burgers in the buns and serve immediately.

GRILLED EGGPLANT WITH SUN-DRIED TOMATO MAYONNAISE ON FRENCH WHEAT HOAGIES

Serves 3

Eggplant is a vegetable that is underutilized in some households, which is too bad because it's delicious, versatile, and good for you. I especially like it grilled, as here, and I jazz up the sandwich by spreading rich Sun-Dried Tomato Mayonnaise on the bread. It's important to leach the excess moisture and bitter flavor from the eggplant by letting it drain for a half-hour or so, as described below. Finally, eggplant may inhibit high levels of blood cholesterol—which makes this vegetable even more desirable.

1 medium eggplant, trimmed and sliced crosswise into ½-inch-thick rounds (about ¾ pound)
1 teaspoon fine sea salt
2 tablespoons olive oil
3 French Wheat Hoagies (page 186), split lengthwise
6 tablespoons Sun-Dried Tomato Mayonnaise (page 114)
¾ cup shredded part-skim mozzarella cheese
Arugula leaves or lettuce leaves

continued

Put the eggplant slices in a colander set on a plate and toss them with the salt. Let stand for about 30 minutes to draw out excess moisture. Rinse the eggplant well and pat dry with paper towels.

Preheat the broiler or prepare a charcoal grill.

Brush both sides of the eggplant slices with oil. Broil or grill the eggplant about 4 inches from the heat, turning once, for about 5 minutes or until browned and tender. Transfer the eggplant to a plate.

Spread the hoagies with the mayonnaise. Place the eggplant on the bottom halves of the hoagies and sprinkle with cheese. Top with arugula leaves and then the top halves of the hoagies. Serve the sandwiches warm or at room temperature.

FALAFEL BURGERS ON 100 PERCENT WHOLE WHEAT BREAD

Serves 6

My falafel is especially wholesome because it's made from a mixture of bulgur and beans and the patties are quickly sautéed, not deep-fried. Bear in mind that you can use either low-fat or nonfat yogurt for the tahini sauce.

1 cup bulgur
Boiling water
2 cups cooked garbanzo beans (see page 143 for instructions for cooking
    beans) or drained and rinsed canned beans
1 small onion, quartered
2 garlic cloves, finely chopped
2 tablespoons plus 2 teaspoons fresh lemon juice
1 teaspoon ground cumin
1 teaspoon salt
1 teaspoon crushed red pepper flakes
1 cup fresh bread crumbs, preferably from 100 Percent Whole Wheat
    Bread (page 199)
2 tablespoons chopped fresh parsley
2 tablespoons chopped fresh cilantro
½ cup plain low-fat yogurt
¼ cup tahini
1 tablespoon chopped fresh mint or parsley
3 tablespoons olive oil
12 slices of 100 Percent Whole Wheat Bread (page 199)
2 plum tomatoes, seeded and chopped
1 medium cucumber, peeled, seeded, and chopped
Chopped lettuce

Put the bulgur in a bowl and pour in enough boiling water to cover by 2 inches.
Let stand, stirring occasionally, for about 20 minutes or until the bulgur is soft

and plump. Drain through a wire sieve, pressing hard on the bulgur to remove excess moisture.

In a food processor fitted with a metal blade, puree the beans, onion, garlic, 2 tablespoons of the lemon juice, cumin, salt, and pepper flakes just until smooth. Scrape down the sides of the workbowl as necessary and do not over-process.

Transfer the bean mixture to a bowl and stir in the bulgur, bread crumbs, parsley, and cilantro. The mixture should be stiff enough to form into patties without sticking to your hands. If not, add more bread crumbs.

Form the mixture into 6 patties each about 3½ inches wide. Set the patties on a waxed paper–lined baking sheet, cover, and refrigerate for 30 minutes.

Blend the yogurt with the tahini, remaining 2 teaspoons of lemon juice, and mint. Set aside.

In a large nonstick skillet, heat the oil over medium heat. Add the patties and cook them for 8 to 10 minutes, turning once, until crisp and golden brown on both sides. Drain on paper towels. Put one each on six slices of bread, then add the tomatoes, cucumbers, and lettuce. Spoon some yogurt-tahini sauce over each sandwich, top with the remaining slices, and serve warm.

GRILLED PIZZA SANDWICH ON GARDEN O' PLENTY BREAD

Serves 2

This open-face sandwich takes unabashed advantage of summer's crop of tomatoes and basil. I highly recommend grilling it over a hot charcoal fire instead of broiling it. The charcoal flavor is one of summer's benefits.

2   slices Garden O' Plenty Bread (page 223)
2   teaspoons extra-virgin olive oil
2   garlic cloves
1   large tomato, thinly sliced
2   tablespoons chopped fresh basil, or 1 teaspoon Italian seasoning
2   ½-ounce slices part-skim mozzarella cheese

Preheat the broiler or prepare a charcoal fire.

Brush both sides of the bread with oil and toast under the broiler or over the charcoal fire for about 3 minutes, turning often, until lightly browned. Rub the hot toast on one side with the garlic. The garlic should disappear into the bread.

Divide the tomato slices evenly between both slices of bread. Sprinkle with basil and then top with the cheese. Broil for about 2 minutes or until the cheese melts. Or put the sandwiches on the sides of the grill away from the coals, cover the grill, and cook for about 2 minutes until the cheese melts. Serve immediately.

CHAPTER
—·—5—·—

Vegetarian Sandwiches

In some ways, these sandwiches are the heart of the book, while the bread recipes remain the soul. The sandwiches on the pages that follow exemplify how I like to eat, getting all my daily nutrients exclusively from plant-based products. I never tire of the produce from the garden and the grocery. When I visit cities that have them, I make regular pilgrimages to the farmers' markets to sample vegetables and fruits I may not be able to grow or buy in rural Montana. And I am always inspired to try something new, or to combine an old favorite with a new infatuation. This curiosity is what makes these purely vegetarian sandwiches so intriguing: some are made with expected combinations of ingredients; others are made with slightly unexpected combinations.

I cannot emphasize strongly enough how important the freshly baked bread is to the overall goodness of the sandwiches. The breads I have selected marry well with the specific ingredients and provide as nice a balance as possible of complex carbohydrates and fiber with vitamins and minerals. The health aspects are vitally important but so is the taste. Try something as simple as Monterey Jack cheese and sweet Vidalia onions on black bread or as fancy as roasted peppers and mozzarella on wheat bread. Both "hit the spot" in terms of taste and nutrition.

Hitting that "spot" is my goal with these recipes. I hope you will agree that with only a little imagination and some fresh ingredients, it's simple to make a healthful sandwich without relying in the least on any meat. Let's hear it for vegetable power!

ROASTED ITALIAN VEGETABLES ON OLD-FASHIONED WHEAT BREAD

Serves 4

The mellowness of the roasted vegetables balances perfectly with the earthy taste of wheat, making this a totally satisfying sandwich. I love the mixture because, while it's best in the summer when the vegetables are in season, you can make it almost any time of year and serve it as a warm, room-temperature, or cold sandwich. I like it spread on crackers, too. The vegetable filling keeps in the refrigerator for a day or two.

continued

1 medium eggplant (about 1 pound), cubed
1 large tomato, quartered
1 medium zucchini, cut into ¾-inch rounds
1 medium red bell pepper, seeded and cut into wedges
1 medium red onion, peeled and quartered
2 garlic cloves, minced
2 tablespoons extra-virgin olive oil
¾ teaspoon sea salt
2 tablespoons chopped fresh basil, or 1½ teaspoons dried
⅜ teaspoon crushed hot red pepper flakes
8 slices Old-Fashioned Wheat Bread (page 181), toasted
¼ cup Pesto Mayonnaise (page 115; optional)

Preheat the oven to 400°F.

Lay the eggplant, tomato, zucchini, pepper, onion, and garlic in a shallow baking pan. Drizzle with olive oil and toss to coat. Sprinkle with salt.

Bake for 45 to 60 minutes or until the eggplant is very soft and the vegetables are lightly browned. Toss the warm vegetables with the basil and hot pepper. Serve warm, let the vegetables cool to room temperature, or chill before serving.

Spread the toasted bread with the Pesto Mayonnaise, if desired. Top 4 slices with the roasted vegetables and then with the remaining 4 slices of bread. Cut into halves and serve.

BEN'S BURGER ON MULTIGRAIN BUNS

Serves 3

I call this a "burger" because it's made on a toasted bun and it pleases my son, Ben, to do so. But what else would I call this zesty sandwich? It's Ben's favorite and I'm happy to make it for him whenever I can, since the tomatoes are a good source of vitamin C and the avocado provides some protein, niacin, and more vitamin C. It's true that avocados are about 15 percent fat, but the fat is in the form of unsaturated vegetable oil.

1 **ripe avocado, pitted and peeled**
1 **teaspoon fresh lemon juice**
⅛ **teaspoon fine sea salt**
3 **Multigrain Buns (page 232), split and toasted**
1 **beefsteak tomato, cut into 6 thick slices**
1 **cup Barbecued Onions (page 126), warm or room temperature**

In a small bowl, mash the avocado with the lemon juice and salt. Spread the avocado on the bottom halves of the toasted buns.

Put 2 tomato slices on each of the buns and spoon ⅓ cup of the onions over the tomatoes. Top with the top halves of the buns and serve immediately.

HERBS 'N' COTTAGE CHEESE ON CARAWAY RYE BREAD

Serves 4

Although I like the creaminess provided by the mayonnaise, you can omit it to save calories; the cottage cheese spread is moist and creamy by itself. It also stands up deliciously to the bold flavors of the Caraway Rye Bread.

½ cup Homemade Yolk-Free Mayonnaise (page 111) or reduced-calorie mayonnaise
8 slices Caraway Rye Bread (page 213)
2 cups Herb 'n' Cottage Cheese Spread (page 118)
Alfalfa sprouts

Spread the mayonnaise on all 8 slices of bread. Spread the cottage cheese mixture evenly on 4 slices, then top with a small handful of sprouts and the remaining slices of bread. Cut into halves and serve.

MONTEREY JACK AND VIDALIA ONION ON RUSSIAN BLACK BREAD

Serves 2

The melted cheese and sweet onion cling to each other between slices of robust black bread to make a satisfying, warm sandwich enlivened with Lemon-Mustard Spread. I especially like to use sweet Vidalia, Walla-Walla, or Maui onions for this sandwich but you may prefer stronger-tasting yellow onions or white Spanish onions.

4 slices of Russian Black Bread (page 217)
3 tablespoons Lemon-Mustard Spread (page 121)
½ cup shredded low-sodium, low-fat Monterey Jack cheese
1 small Vidalia onion, thinly sliced

Preheat the broiler.

Toast the bread on both sides under the broiler. Spread 2 slices with Lemon-Mustard Spread and then sprinkle them with cheese. Broil for about 1 minute or until the cheese melts.

Take the sandwiches from the broiler, top the melted cheese with onion, and then add the remaining slices of bread. Cut into halves and serve.

WALDORF SALAD ON LEMON BREAD

Serves 2

Have you ever thought of eating a Waldorf salad between two slices of bread? This healthful version, bound by nonfat yogurt instead of mayonnaise, tastes especially good with light Lemon Bread.

2 medium Granny Smith apples, cored, unpeeled
1 celery rib
¼ cup chopped walnuts
¼ cup raisins
1 tablespoon honey
2 tablespoons plain nonfat yogurt
2 tablespoons low-fat mayonnaise
4 slices Lemon Bread (page 194)

In a food processor, grate the apples and celery. Transfer to a bowl and stir in the walnuts, raisins, honey, yogurt, and mayonnaise. Spread the mixture evenly on 2 slices of bread and top with the remaining slices of bread. Cut into halves and serve.

VEGETARIAN DREAM SANDWICH ON SPELT BREAD

Serves 2

I call this a "dream" sandwich because while it's a typical vegetarian combo (tomatoes, onions, avocados, and sprouts), you can make it to suit your own tastes by adding a slice of low-sodium Swiss cheese, a few pieces of crisp turkey bacon, or some canned tuna. I have tailored it to fit my needs by spreading a little Lemon-Mustard Spread on nutritious, fortifying Spelt Bread. Radish sprouts are noticeably more peppery than alfalfa sprouts.

2 tablespoons Lemon-Mustard Spread (page 121)
4 slices Spelt Bread (page 226)
1 medium tomato, sliced
5 to 6 large, thin slices red onion
1 avocado, peeled, pitted, and sliced
Radish or alfalfa sprouts

Spread the Lemon-Mustard Spread on 2 slices of bread. Arrange the tomato, onion, and avocado slices on the bread. Top with sprouts and then with the remaining bread. Cut into halves and serve.

TOFU CHEESE-AVOCADO SANDWICH ON GARDEN O' PLENTY BREAD

Serves 2

I highly recommend this bread for folks who really like their vegetables. There are nearly as many veggies baked into the bread as there are packed between the slices. Be sure the avocado is ripe before mashing it; you can tell if the fruit yields at all when pressed between your fingers. Tofu cheese is made from protein-rich tofu and often is flavored like cheese. Buy it in natural foods stores.

1 large avocado, peeled and pitted
¼ teaspoon fine sea salt
½ teaspoon salt-free herb and spice blend
4 slices Garden O' Plenty Bread (page 223)
4 radishes, thinly sliced
⅓ cup shredded tofu cheese
½ cup Barbecued Onions (page 126), cooled
Green leaf lettuce

In a small bowl, mash the avocado, salt, and herb and spice blend with the back of a fork. Spread the mixture on 2 slices of bread.

Arrange the sliced radishes, tofu cheese, and Barbecued Onions on top of the avocado. Top with lettuce leaves and then with the remaining bread. Cut into halves and serve.

BLACK BEANS AND SALSA ON MULTIGRAIN BREAD

Serves 2

Beans are a terrific source of fiber and protein, and I find black beans especially flavorful. Here I mix them with salsa for a taste of the Southwest.

½ cup cooked black beans (see page 143 for cooking instructions) or drained canned black beans
½ cup Homemade Salsa (page 117)
Fine sea salt
Freshly ground pepper (optional)
4 slices Multigrain Bread (page 201)
2 tablespoons Homemade Yolk-Free Mayonnaise (page 111) or reduced-calorie mayonnaise
Alfalfa sprouts

In a small bowl, mash the beans with the salsa using the back of a fork. Season to taste with salt and pepper.

Spread all 4 slices of bread with mayonnaise. Spread the black bean mixture on 2 slices, then top with sprouts, and the remaining bread, mayonnaise side down. Cut into halves and serve.

CUCUMBER SALAD IN YOGURT CHEESE ON BASIC WHITE BREAD

Serves 4

Cucumber and yogurt salad is deliciously refreshing but does require time for the yogurt to drain and thicken and the cucumbers to drain and expel extra moisture. Otherwise, the salad will be a soggy mess!

1½ cups plain low-fat yogurt
2 medium cucumbers, peeled, seeded and cut crosswise into ¼-inch-thick
     slices
½ teaspoon fine sea salt
2 tablespoons finely chopped red onion
1 teaspoon dried dill
½ teaspoon ground cumin
Freshly ground pepper
4 slices Basic White Bread (page 184)
2 green leaf lettuce leaves
2 large tomato slices, quartered

Set a wire mesh strainer over a bowl. Line the strainer with paper towels. Put the yogurt in the strainer and fold the excess paper towels over it to cover. Set a coffee mug on top of the paper towels to weight the yogurt. Let stand for 1 hour. Liquid will drain into the bowl.

Put the cucumbers in a colander and set the colander on a plate. Toss the cucumbers with the salt and let stand for 1 hour. After 1 hour, rinse and drain the cucumbers. In batches, squeeze the cucumbers in a kitchen towel to remove excess moisture.

Discard the liquid from the yogurt or reserve to use in soup. Remove the thickened yogurt from the paper towels and put in a bowl. Mix with the onion, dill, cumin, and pepper to taste.

Place the lettuce leaves and tomatoes on 4 slices of bread. Spoon on the cucumber salad, top with the remaining slices, and serve immediately.

MUSHROOM-WALNUT SPREAD ON MULTIGRAIN BREAD

Serves 4

Blending finely chopped mushrooms and walnuts with soft, light cream cheese (Neufchâtel) results in a rich, filling sandwich. Try this spread on crackers for a snack or party hors d'oeuvre.

10 ounces fresh mushrooms
4 ounces Neufchâtel cheese, at room temperature
½ cup finely chopped walnuts
2 scallions, finely chopped
1 tablespoon fresh lemon juice
1 teaspoon dried dill
½ teaspoon fine sea salt
¼ teaspoon freshly ground pepper
8 slices Multigrain Bread (page 201)

Using a food processor fitted with the metal blade, process the mushrooms until very finely chopped but not to a paste. Alternatively, chop the mushrooms with a sharp knife. Transfer the mushrooms to a bowl.

Add the cheese, walnuts, scallions, lemon juice, dill, salt, and pepper to the bowl with the mushrooms. Use a rubber spatula to mix the ingredients together into a spreadable mixture.

Spread the mushroom mixture evenly on 4 slices of bread. Top with the remaining slices of bread. Cut into halves and serve.

ROASTED RED PEPPERS
WITH MOZZARELLA
ON SALT-FREE WHEAT BREAD
Serves 4

This sandwich is testament to the theory that less is more: it's a simple concoction of roasted peppers, vinegar, and cheese. I use Pesto Mayonnaise to heighten the flavors further, but you could substitute ordinary or French-Style Yolk-Free Mayonnaise (page 112) instead. Use any wheat bread you prefer; I chose Salt-Free as a way to reduce the amount of salt in the overall sandwich. And, for a splurge, try fresh mozzarella cheese. More calories but more taste, too.

4 red bell peppers
8 slices Salt-Free Wheat Bread (page 230)
4 tablespoons Pesto Mayonnaise (page 115)
4 teaspoons balsamic or cider vinegar
6 ounces part-skim mozzarella cheese, thinly sliced

Position a broiler rack 4 inches from the source of heat and preheat the broiler. Broil the peppers for about 15 minutes, turning often, until charred on all sides. Put the charred peppers in a paper bag and let them cool for about 10 minutes. Using the back of a knife, scrape and peel the charred skin. Rinse the peppers under running water to remove all specks of charred skin, if you wish. Stem and seed the peppers.

continued

Spread the bread slices with Pesto Mayonnaise. Place a roasted pepper on each of 4 slices. Sprinkle each with vinegar and top with slices of cheese and then the remaining bread, spread side down. Serve immediately.

SUMMER GARDEN SANDWICH ON MULTIGRAIN BUNS
Serves 4

This delicious sandwich is custom-made for a summer's day. It calls for lush, vine-ripened tomatoes and fresh, tender zucchini. Keep in mind that a fresh tomato has about 50 percent of the recommended daily allowance of vitamin C—another good reason for eating this sandwich as often as possible!

6 tablespoons Oil and Vinegar Dressing
4 Multigrain Buns (page 232), split
2 large tomatoes, sliced
1 medium zucchini, thinly sliced
1 small green bell pepper, cut into rings
7 to 8 small red onion rings
Red leaf lettuce

Sprinkle 1½ tablespoons of dressing over the cut sides of each bun. Arrange the tomatoes, zucchini, pepper rings, and onion rings on the bottom halves of each bun. Top with lettuce leaves and then the top halves of the buns. Serve immediately.

CHAPTER
—·-6—·-

Sweet and Savory
Tea Sandwiches

There are only a handful of sandwiches in this chapter, but each one is a perfect gem and illustrates the old saying about good things coming in small packages. I call them tea sandwiches because, to my way of thinking, these treasures are meant for quiet celebrations, such as tea parties. But many are equally good served with midmorning coffee or an early evening glass of wine or cider. And some do very well for breakfast or lunch.

Most of the following sandwiches are made with fruit. This may seem odd. After all, who ever heard of a fruit sandwich? In fact, fruit tastes very good nestled between two slices of bread, particularly when partnered with nut butter or the low-fat cream cheese called Neufchâtel. Take a bite of the apricot and pecan mixture on Lemon Bread or the cranberry-orange-banana team served on Banana-Nut Bread. Both are sweet and delicious, providing great flavor, lots of vitamins, minerals, and fiber and something else: sensory novelty. Your taste buds are not expecting these flavors. I think it's commendable to exercise them now and again. These sandwiches provide an exhilarating workout.

Remember that while I have written the recipes with yields reflecting that one sandwich serves one person, there is nothing to stop you from cutting them into small squares or rectangles to increase the number of people each recipe will feed.

HERBED CREAM CHEESE
ON SPELT BREAD

Serves 4 to 6

This full-flavored vegetable spread makes a wonderful sandwich that is delicious with afternoon tea but is equally tasty for lunch at school or work. Make the spread as spicy as you want by altering the type of salsa. I also serve the spread as a dip for raw vegetables; it makes about 1¾ cups of spread.

8 ounces Neufchâtel cheese, softened
¼ cup shredded or finely chopped radishes
¼ cup pitted and chopped black olives
⅓ cup pitted and chopped green olives
1 small cucumber, seeded and chopped
2 tablespoons Homemade Salsa (page 117) or commercial salsa
½ teaspoon salt-free herb and spice blend
Fine sea salt
Freshly ground pepper
8 slices Spelt Bread (page 226)
Alfalfa sprouts or shredded lettuce

Mix the cheese with the radishes, olives, cucumber, salsa, herb and spice blend, and salt and pepper to taste. Spread the cheese mixture evenly on 4 slices of bread. Top each sandwich with sprouts or lettuce and then with the remaining 4 slices of bread. Cut into halves or quarters and serve.

APPLES AND DATES
ON APPLE SPICE TOAST

Serves 2

I really enjoy the textural contrast of a crisp apple and soft, sweet date, and when the two are together between Apple Spice Bread, the result is a delightful sandwich that is at home on both the tea table and breakfast table. I call for Medjhool dates, grown in Arizona and California and the biggest, plumpest dates on the market. They also are more costly than Deglet Noor dates, which work well, too, in this sandwich. Make sure dates are moist and soft when you buy them.

2 tablespoons Cinnamon Spread (page 125)
4 slices Apple Spice Bread (page 221), lightly toasted
1 large apple, peeled, cored, and thinly sliced
½ cup Medjhool dates, sliced (about 3 ounces)

Spread the Cinnamon Spread lightly on each slice of toast. Top 2 slices with apples and dates and then with the remaining slices of toast. Cut into halves and serve.

ALMOND BUTTER AND BANANAS ON APPLE SPICE BREAD

Serves 2

Here's a fantastic tea sandwich that relies on fresh fruit and sugarless preserves for sweetness. Almond butter is sold in natural foods stores and tastes sublime spread on moist Apple Spice Bread. It also is a terrific source of protein, as are bananas of potassium.

⅓ cup natural almond butter
4 slices Apple Spice Bread (page 221)
1 medium banana, sliced
Alfalfa sprouts (optional)
¼ cup sugarless blueberry preserves

Spread almond butter evenly on 2 slices of bread. Top each with sliced banana and then sprouts, if desired. Spread preserves evenly on remaining 2 slices of bread and then place them, preserves side down, on top of the bananas and almond butter. Cut into halves and serve.

STRAWBERRIES, DATES, AND ALMOND BUTTER ON OATMEAL SPICE BREAD

Serves 2

It may sound wacky to put sliced fresh strawberries between two pieces of bread, but why not? When paired with sticky, sweet dates, the two simulate the flavor and texture of jam—but without any added sugar. Plus, the fruit provides valuable fiber. Full-flavored Oatmeal Spice Bread stars in that role, too.

4 slices Oatmeal Spice Bread (page 207)
½ cup natural almond butter
¼ cup finely chopped dates
1 cup thinly sliced ripe strawberries

Spread all 4 slices of bread with almond butter. Sprinkle 2 slices with dates, pressing lightly so the dates adhere. Top with sliced strawberries and then with the remaining slices of bread, almond-butter side down. Cut into halves and serve.

PINEAPPLE-PEACH-PECAN SANDWICH ON CINNAMON-RAISIN BREAD

Serves 4

Crunchy nuts and sweet, juicy pineapple and peaches taste just right combined with smooth low-fat cream cheese and cradled between slices of rich Cinnamon-Raisin Bread. This fruit sandwich is great for breakfast, lunch, a snack, or light supper.

8 ounces Neufchâtel cheese, softened
¼ cup chopped pecans
1 8-ounce can unsweetened crushed pineapple, drained
8 slices Cinnamon-Raisin Bread (page 192)
2 peaches, pitted, peeled, and thinly sliced
4 green leaf lettuce leaves

In a small bowl, mix the cheese, nuts, and pineapple. Spread on 4 slices of bread and then top each of these slices with peach slices. Lay lettuce leaves on top of the peaches and then top the sandwiches with the remaining bread. Cut into halves and serve.

CRANBERRY SPREAD WITH ORANGES ON BANANA-NUT BREAD

Serves 3

Sugar-free cranberry sauce is tart and tasty but cries out to be paired with naturally sweet foods such as oranges and Banana-Nut Bread. I buy it in natural foods stores, although it's available in some specialty shops, too. Cranberries are potent fruits, touted for their antibiotic properties, especially for combating urinary tract infections. They also may play a role in preventing kidney stones.

8 ounces Neufchâtel cheese, softened
½ cup sugar-free cranberry sauce
6 slices Banana-Nut Bread (page 210)
2 oranges, peeled and cut crosswise into thin slices
Watercress sprigs

In a small bowl, mix the cheese and cranberry sauce. Spread on 3 slices of bread and then top each of these slices with orange slices. Lay watercress sprigs on top of the oranges and then top the sandwiches with the remaining bread. Cut into halves and serve.

PEANUT BUTTER, BANANA, AND GRANOLA ON MULTIGRAIN BREAD

Serves 2

When you need a sandwich to keep you going, try this one. The peanut butter and granola are both mighty nutritious and mighty filling. The apple butter and banana provide vitamins and valuable potassium. Pack these sandwiches for a day hike or canoe trip. I promise they will "hit the spot."

4 tablespoons natural peanut butter
4 slices Multigrain Bread (page 201)
2 tablespoons natural apple butter
¼ cup Granola (page 145)
1 large banana, thinly sliced

Spread the peanut butter on 2 slices of bread. Spread the apple butter on the other 2 slices.

Sprinkle the peanut butter–spread bread with granola, pressing gently so that the granola adheres to the peanut butter. Lay banana slices on top of the granola. Top with the remaining slices of bread, apple-butter side down, cut into halves, and serve.

NEUFCHÂTEL CHEESE AND CHIVES ON PUMPERNICKEL BREAD

Serves 2

I hope you will try this with fresh chives—they make a big difference in the final flavor of the low-fat cream cheese filling. The lemon juice and herb and spice blend compensate for salt while providing their own good flavors, too.

4 ounces Neufchâtel cheese, softened
2 tablespoons chopped fresh chives, or 2 teaspoons dried
1 tablespoon fresh lemon juice
½ teaspoon salt-free herb and spice blend
Freshly ground pepper
4 slices Pumpernickel Bread (page 215)
1 small cucumber, thinly sliced
Alfalfa sprouts

In a small bowl, mash the cheese with the chives, lemon juice, herb and spice blend, and pepper to taste. Spread the mixture on 2 slices of bread. Top with cucumber slices and sprouts, and then with the remaining 2 slices of bread. Cut into halves and serve.

APRICOT-AND-PECAN CREAM CHEESE SANDWICH ON LEMON BREAD

Serves 2

This is a rich, crunchy sandwich made with Neufchâtel cheese—low-fat cream cheese that is approximately 30 percent lower in fat than other cream cheese. Without a doubt, that's a substantial savings, but still does not qualify Neufchâtel for "health food" status. Go easy with it.

4 ounces Neufchâtel cheese, softened
4 slices Lemon Bread (page 194)
¼ cup chopped pecans
6 tablespoons sugarless apricot preserves

Spread the Neufchâtel cheese evenly on 2 slices of bread. Top with pecans, pressing lightly so that the nuts adhere. Spread the preserves on the remaining 2 slices and then put them, preserves side down, on top of the nuts. Cut into halves and serve.

CHAPTER
—·—7—·—

Spreads, Dressings, and Garnishes

This chapter has twenty-one short recipes that are long on punch. Without them, sandwiches would be arguably humdrum, but with them they are lively, exciting, and bold. Big claims, perhaps, but I think accurate ones. When I put Lemon-Mustard Spread or Pesto Mayonnaise on homemade bread and then fill it with other ingredients, the mingling flavors sing in joyous concert. When I top an avocado sandwich or turkey franks with Barbecued Onions, the meal takes on tangy new dimensions.

I have included recipes in this chapter for yolk-free mayonnaise, homemade catsup, mustard, and salsa. I also have chunky guacamole, a smooth bean spread, my own barbecue sauce, and lots more. Don't feel shy about using these with sandwiches of your own devising, or, when appropriate, in salads or as dips for raw vegetables or corn chips. Think of these recipes as fanciful building blocks that give sandwiches the zest and zing they need to be endlessly intriguing.

HOMEMADE YOLK-FREE MAYONNAISE

Makes about 1 cup

I prefer this fresh-tasting, rich version of homemade mayonnaise to anything available in a jar. It takes only minutes to concoct, but what a difference it makes on a sandwich! Using liquid egg substitute eliminates concern about raw eggs and the possibility of contamination by salmonella bacteria. Be sure the egg substitute is at room temperature—if it's cold it won't work in the recipe. To bring it to room temperature, set a small bowl of egg substitute in a larger bowl of hot tap water. Stir the egg substitute for about two minutes, until tepid.

¼ **cup liquid egg substitute, at room temperature**
2 **tablespoons fresh lemon juice**
½ **teaspoon fine sea salt**
½ **teaspoon dry mustard**
¾ **cup canola oil**
Freshly ground pepper

Put the egg substitute, lemon juice, salt, and mustard into a blender. Cover and blend for 5 seconds.

With the blender running on medium, remove the lid and slowly add the oil in a steady stream. This should take about 45 seconds, by which time the mayonnaise will thicken. Season to taste with pepper.

Use right away or transfer to a lidded container. Refrigerate for up to 3 days.

FRENCH-STYLE
YOLK-FREE MAYONNAISE

Makes about 1 cup

This recipe is almost identical to the preceding one, except I have substituted ¼ cup of extra-virgin olive oil for some of the canola oil. This gives the mayonnaise a fruity flavor reminiscent of those made in France.

¼ **cup liquid egg substitute, at room temperature**
2 **tablespoons fresh lemon juice**
½ **teaspoon fine sea salt**
½ **teaspoon dry mustard**
¼ **cup extra-virgin olive oil**
½ **cup canola oil**
Freshly ground pepper

Put the egg substitute, lemon juice, salt, and mustard into a blender. Cover and blend for 5 seconds.

With the blender running on medium, remove the lid and slowly add the oils in a steady stream. This should take about 45 seconds, by which time the mayonnaise will thicken. Season to taste with pepper.

Use right away or transfer to a lidded container. Refrigerate for up to 3 days.

HERB YOLK-FREE MAYONNAISE

Makes about 1 cup

Again, this is basically a variation on my recipe for mayonnaise made with liquid egg substitute rather than whole eggs, but I think the spread is so *good*, I can't stop playing with the master recipe. In this version I stir in a good measure of fresh herbs. Use your favorite, or a combination of herbs. It will make your sandwiches sing with fresh flavor!

¼ cup liquid egg substitute, at room temperature
2 tablespoons fresh lemon juice
½ teaspoon fine sea salt
½ teaspoon dry mustard
¾ cup canola oil
Freshly ground pepper
4 tablespoons chopped fresh herbs, such as parsley, tarragon, oregano, or
    dill; or 1 tablespoon dried herbs

Put the egg substitute, lemon juice, salt, and mustard into a blender. Cover and blend for 5 seconds.

With the blender running on medium, remove the lid and slowly add the oil in a steady stream. This should take about 45 seconds, by which time the mayonnaise will thicken. Season to taste with pepper. Stir in the herbs.

Use right away or transfer to a lidded container. Refrigerate for up to 3 days.

SUN-DRIED TOMATO MAYONNAISE

Makes about ¾ cup

These pungent tomatoes add bold color and a Mediterranean flavor to lots of dishes, and are especially good mixed with mayonnaise. The dehydrated, oil-free sort in plastic packages are sold in many supermarkets and specialty stores. If you can only find oil-packed sun-dried tomatoes, rinse them under hot, running water and then pat them dry before pureeing them. Toss about ¼ cup of chopped basil and 1 pressed garlic clove into the mayonnaise and use it as a vegetable dip.

½ cup sun-dried tomato halves, *not* packed in oil (about 2½ ounces)
½ cup Homemade Yolk-Free Mayonnaise (page 111) or reduced-calorie
    mayonnaise

Put the tomatoes in a small bowl and pour in enough boiling water to cover. Let them stand until softened, about ten minutes. Drain and pat well with paper towels.

Put the soaked tomatoes in a blender or food processor fitted with the metal blade and process until smooth. If necessary, add a tablespoon or so of mayonnaise to the blender or processor to lubricate the tomatoes so they puree smoothly. Transfer the puree to a bowl and stir in the mayonnaise. Use immediately or cover and refrigerate for up to 1 week.

PESTO MAYONNAISE

Makes about 1 cup

Try this pesto-flavored mayonnaise on tomato or other vegetable sandwiches. Or stir some into potato or pasta salad.

¼ cup liquid egg substitute, at room temperature
2 tablespoons fresh lemon juice
½ teaspoon fine sea salt
½ teaspoon dry mustard
3 tablespoons Pesto (page 116)
¾ cup canola oil
Freshly ground pepper

Put the egg substitute, lemon juice, salt, mustard, and pesto into a blender. Cover and blend for 5 seconds.

With the blender running on medium, remove the lid and slowly add the oil in a steady stream. This should take about 45 seconds, by which time the mayonnaise will thicken. Season to taste with pepper.

Use right away or transfer to a lidded container. Refrigerate for up to 3 days.

PESTO

Makes about 1 cup

Traditional pesto is made with copious amounts of olive oil, and while olive oil is a monounsaturated oil and therefore preferable to other oils, it is high in calories. In this recipe I use only enough olive oil for good flavor and texture. You will also notice that I omit pine nuts or walnuts, two ingredients in most pesto recipes, but which are high in fat. The healthy amounts of basil and garlic more than make up for their absence.

2 cups tightly packed basil leaves
3 large garlic cloves, chopped
⅓ cup extra-virgin olive oil
½ cup freshly grated Parmesan cheese
Fine sea salt

Put the basil and garlic in a blender. With the blender running on medium, slowly add the olive oil until the basil is pureed and the sauce is smooth. Transfer to a bowl and stir in the cheese. Season to taste with salt.

Refrigerate the pesto in a lidded container for up to 3 days.

HOMEMADE SALSA

Makes about 1 cup

Although you can buy jars of prepared salsa in every supermarket and grocery in the country (it has surpassed catsup as the "condiment of choice" for Americans), I prefer to make my own. This way, I know precisely what is in it and I know it's as fresh as can be. You can vary the ingredients to suit your own tastes, but this mixture works very well.

6 ripe plum tomatoes or 1 pound vine-ripened tomatoes, seeded and
      chopped
2 tablespoons finely chopped onion
1 garlic clove, minced
1 jalapeño chile, seeded and finely chopped
1 tablespoon fresh lime juice
½ teaspoon fine sea salt
2 tablespoons chopped fresh cilantro or parsley

In a medium bowl, gently toss together all the ingredients. Cover and refrigerate for at least 1 hour or up to 24 hours.

HERB 'N' COTTAGE CHEESE SPREAD

Makes about 2 cups

Adding generous amounts of fresh, chopped vegetables to low-fat cottage cheese converts a humdrum food into a special one. I particularly like this between two slices of Caraway Rye Bread (page 213).

1 cup low-fat cottage cheese
2 tablespoons chopped onion
2 tablespoons chopped green bell pepper
2 tablespoons chopped celery
1 tablespoon snipped fresh chives or 1 teaspoon dried

Mix all ingredients in a bowl. Use right away or store, covered, in the refrigerator.

DILL-HERB SPREAD

Makes about 2 cups

As good as this is as a spread, it is equally fabulous as a dip for vegetables or Oven-Baked Tortilla Chips (page 123). Be careful you use dried dillweed and not the far stronger dill seeds.

2 cups plain low-fat yogurt
¾ cup Homemade Yolk-Free Mayonnaise (page 111) or reduced-calorie
    mayonnaise
½ cup snipped fresh chives, or 3 tablespoons dried
1 tablespoon minced onion
3 tablespoons chopped fresh parsley
2 teaspoons dried dill
1½ teaspoons salt-free herb and spice blend
2 garlic cloves, pressed
Fine sea salt
Freshly ground pepper

Put the yogurt in a cheesecloth-lined strainer set over a bowl. Drain for 8 hours or overnight in the refrigerator. You will have approximately 1 cup of yogurt "cheese." Discard the liquid in the bowl.

    Using a spoon, gently stir the mayonnaise, chives, onion, parsley, dill, herb and spice blend, and garlic into the yogurt cheese. Be gentle—vigorous stirring or whisking may cause the yogurt to separate. Season to taste with salt and pepper. Refrigerate in a lidded glass jar for up to 5 days.

TANGY YOGURT SPREAD

Makes about 1½ cups

I really am thrilled with this fat-free spread. It packs a lot of flavor with so few calories, getting its tang from a good dose of lemon juice as well as onion and garlic. I like to use lemon juice in place of salt whenever possible—it's a good substitute in many preparations. In this recipe I add only a half-teaspoon of salt.

2　cups plain nonfat yogurt
3　tablespoons fresh lemon juice
4　tablespoons minced onion
4　tablespoons finely chopped fresh parsley
1　teaspoon paprika
½　teaspoon fine sea salt
1　garlic clove, minced

Put the yogurt in a cheesecloth-lined strainer set over a bowl. Drain for 8 hours or overnight in the refrigerator. You will have approximately 1 cup of yogurt "cheese." Discard the liquid in the bowl.

　　Using a spoon, gently stir the remaining ingredients into the yogurt cheese. Be careful—vigorous stirring or whisking may cause the yogurt to separate. Refrigerate in a lidded glass jar for up to 3 days.

LEMON-MUSTARD SPREAD

Makes about 2 cups

This mayonnaise-based spread sparks up everyday tuna or seafood salad. Keep the recipe on file for those times you want a dipping sauce for steamed asparagus or artichokes. For a lighter version, make this with ¾ cup yogurt cheese (see recipes for Dill-Herb Spread and Tangy Yogurt Spread [pages 119 and 120], for information on making yogurt cheese) and ¾ cup mayonnaise.

1½ cups reduced-calorie mayonnaise
4 tablespoons spicy brown mustard
2 tablespoons fresh lemon juice
1 tablespoon grated lemon zest
1 tablespoon honey
Dash of cayenne pepper

Mix all the ingredients well. Refrigerate in a tightly lidded container for up to 1 week.

CREAMY BEAN SPREAD

Makes about 2 cups

When I call for beans I mean legumes (not green beans), the sort that are sold dried or canned. Inexpensive, versatile, and filling, beans are a staple in our house. We also like them because they are high in fiber, vitamins (vitamin A and some B vitamins), calcium, and when mixed with grains, become a complete protein. Here, I use cooked beans in this zesty spread that does double duty as a dip for oven-baked tortilla chips or raw vegetables.

1   teaspoon canola oil
1   medium onion, chopped
1   jalapeño or serrano chile, seeded and minced
2   garlic cloves, crushed
1   cup cooked Anasazi, pinto, or other beans (see page 143 for cooking
      instructions) or drained canned beans
2   tablespoons fresh lemon juice
1   teaspoon low-sodium tamari
1   teaspoon salt-free herb and spice blend
Approximately ¼ cup cooking liquid or liquid from canned beans
¼ cup chopped fresh cilantro or parsley

In a medium nonstick skillet, heat the oil. Add the onion, chile, and garlic and cook over medium heat for about 5 minutes or until the onion is softened.

Transfer the vegetables to a food processor fitted with the metal blade. Add the beans, lemon juice, tamari, and herb and spice blend. Process until smooth.

Add the liquid, a tablespoon at a time, if necessary for a spreadable consistency.

Scrape the bean spread into a bowl and stir in the cilantro or parsley by hand. Use immediately or refrigerate, covered, for 2 to 3 days.

OVEN-BAKED TORTILLA CHIPS

Makes about 2 dozen chips

These are especially good dipped into the Creamy Bean Spread on page 122. The chips are salt-free and far less greasy and fattening than commercial chips.

3–4 uncooked corn tortillas

Preheat the oven to 375°F.

Spray both sides of the tortillas with nonstick cooking spray. Cut each tortilla into six wedges. Lay the wedges on an ungreased baking sheet (you may need 2) and bake for 10 to 15 minutes or until crisp. Turn the wedges once during baking. Let the chips cool completely on the baking sheet. Serve right away or store in an airtight container for 1 to 2 days.

GUACAMOLE

Makes about 2 cups

I find that black, pebbly-skinned Haas avocados are the best for guacamole because they have better flavor and texture than the larger, smooth-skinned Florida fruit. Authentic guacamole is meant to be chunky, so do not be tempted to make this in a blender or food processor. Use guacamole sparingly—as delicious and healthful as it is, a single avocado has nearly 350 calories. Also, be sure to use ripe avocados, which yield to slight pressure when ready to eat. And depending on your taste preferences, go easy with the jalapeño.

2 ripe avocados, peeled and pitted
¼ cup chopped onion
1 small tomato, peeled, seeded, and chopped
½ to 1 jalapeño chile, seeded and minced
1 tablespoon fresh lime juice
½ teaspoon fine sea salt
2 tablespoons chopped fresh cilantro (optional)
1 garlic clove, pressed

In a medium bowl, coarsely mash the avocado with the back of a fork. Stir in the remaining ingredients. Make sure the garlic is thoroughly crushed. Serve immediately or lay a piece of plastic directly on the guacamole and refrigerate for up to 1 day.

CINNAMON SPREAD

Makes about 1 cup

My children like this spread on toast in the morning. While it contains butter, a little goes a long way in terms of taste. The sweet spread is also good on toast or rolls late in the afternoon or just before bed with a cup of herbal tea.

4 tablespoons (½ stick) unsalted butter, softened
½ cup honey
½ cup powdered whey or powdered milk
1 tablespoon ground cinnamon
1½ teaspoons grated orange zest
¼ teaspoon vanilla extract

Combine all the ingredients and mix well. Use right away or refrigerate for up to 3 days. Let the spread return to room temperature before using.

BARBECUED ONIONS

Makes about 1½ cups

I suggest using this tangy onion topping on several sandwiches throughout the book. You can also use it as a filling in its own right. Spread it and a generous handful of sprouts between two pieces of hearty bread for a quick, delicious meal.

2 large sweet red onions, sliced ¼ inch thick
1 cup Homemade Barbecue Sauce (page 127)

Spray a medium nonstick skillet with nonstick cooking spray. Cook the onions, covered, over medium heat for about 8 minutes or until softened. Uncover and cook for about 5 minutes longer, stirring often, until lightly browned.

Stir in the barbecue sauce and cook for 5 minutes. Use right away or refrigerate in a covered container for up to 5 days.

HOMEMADE BARBECUE SAUCE

Makes about 3 cups

Once you take the time to make a batch of this sauce you will find countless uses for it—those suggested throughout the book as well as just about any time you fire up the backyard grill. Unlike other versions, this is made with catsup sweetened only with a little honey and containing very little salt. To my way of thinking, this is a lot better for you, but with no sacrifice in flavor and intensity. If you find it easier to buy the catsup rather than make your own, look for low-sodium catsup in natural foods stores. An increasing number of supermarkets carry it, too.

2 tablespoons canola oil
1 large onion, finely chopped
2 garlic cloves, minced
2 cups Homemade Spicy Catsup (page 129) or low-sodium honey-
    sweetened commercial catsup
⅓ cup cider vinegar
¼ cup honey
2 tablespoons unsulfured molasses
2 tablespoons spicy brown mustard
2 tablespoons Worcestershire sauce
Tabasco or other hot sauce

In a medium saucepan, heat the oil over medium-low heat. Cook the onion and garlic for about 5 minutes or until softened. Stir in the remaining ingredients, adding Tabasco or hot sauce to taste.

continued

Simmer over low heat for about 30 minutes or until slightly thickened. Let the sauce cool completely before storing in a lidded glass jar for up to 2 weeks.

QUICK HOMEMADE CATSUP

Makes about 1 cup

Making your own catsup may seem fussy. After all, commercial catsups are pretty tasty, right? In fact, they are loaded with sugar, salt, and preservatives that your homemade version is happily without. And by adjusting the seasonings, you can make it exactly as your family likes it. My family likes this version.

¾ **cup low-sodium tomato paste**
2 **tablespoons cider vinegar**
3 **tablespoons honey**
2 **tablespoons water**
1 **teaspoon low-sodium tamari or soy sauce**

Mix all the ingredients in a small saucepan. Bring to a simmer, lower the heat, and cook gently for about 3 minutes.

Let the catsup cool completely before storing in a lidded glass jar for up to 2 weeks.

SPICY HOMEMADE CATSUP

Makes about 2 cups

The addition of onions, garlic, peppers, and an array of herbs and spices makes this catsup a little more forceful than the Quick Homemade Catsup on page 128, but in a delicious sort of way. The flavors mellow after it sits for a day or two.

1 28-ounce can low-sodium crushed tomatoes
5 tablespoons honey
3 tablespoons cider vinegar
2 tablespoons medium chopped onion
1½ teaspoons sweet pepper flakes
1 teaspoon fine sea salt
2 teaspoons salt-free herb and spice blend
⅛ teaspoon ground allspice
½ bay leaf
2 garlic cloves, pressed

Mix all the ingredients in a medium saucepan. Bring to a simmer and cook gently for 45 to 60 minutes, stirring occasionally, or until the mixture reduces by half.

Remove the bay leaf and let the catsup cool for about 10 minutes. Spoon into a blender and blend for 30 seconds or until smooth. Pour into a glass jar and cool completely. Cover and refrigerate for up to 2 weeks.

HOMEMADE MUSTARD

Makes about ¾ cup

This mustard is a pleasing combination of traditional American picnic-table yellow and spicy dark European-style mustard. For honey mustard, stir ¼ cup of honey into the mustard after it cools.

¼ cup mustard seeds
¼ cup dry mustard
½ cup hot water
¾ cup cider vinegar
½ cup water
1 teaspoon salt
1 teaspoon turmeric
¼ teaspoon ground allspice
1 small onion, chopped
1 garlic clove, pressed

In a small bowl, stir together the mustard seeds, dry mustard, and hot water. Let stand for 3 hours.

Combine the vinegar, water, salt, turmeric, allspice, onion, and garlic in a saucepan and cook over medium heat for about 10 minutes or until the liquid is reduced by half. Strain the cooked mixture into the bowl containing the soaked mustard seeds. Stir to combine.

Transfer the mixture to a blender or food processor fitted with the metal blade. Process until coarsely ground.

Put the mustard in the top of a double boiler and cook over simmering water, stirring constantly, for about 10 minutes or until the mixture is thick but still fluid. The mustard will thicken further as it cools. When completely cool, transfer to a lidded container and refrigerate for up to 2 weeks.

CRISPY CROUTONS
Makes about 2½ cups

Baking cubes of bread that have been lightly coated with oil in a slow oven assures that the finished croutons will be evenly browned and crispy all the way through. Sprinkle them in soups or salads—anytime you want a little crunch.

1½ tablespoons canola oil
2 garlic cloves, pressed
2½ cups fresh, ½-inch bread cubes (about 4 slices)
2 tablespoons grated Parmesan cheese
1 tablespoon dried parsley
½ teaspoon salt-free herb and spice blend or Italian seasoning

Preheat the oven to 250°F.

Mix together the oil and garlic. Put the bread cubes in a shallow baking pan and pour the oil-garlic mixture over them. Toss to coat. Sprinkle the cubes with cheese, parsley, and herb and spice blend. Toss well and when the cubes are coated, spread them in a single layer in the pan.

Bake for 45 minutes to 1 hour, tossing occasionally, until the bread cubes are browned and crispy. Transfer to another pan to cool completely. Store in an airtight jar or use immediately.

CHAPTER
—·—8—·—

Basics

This chapter is called "Basics" because it's essential for the success of many of the recipes. Here are the recipes that explain how to prepare some of the foods that eventually end up between slices of bread or in the soup pot. These are very basic cooking methods for roasting, poaching, and stock making, among others. The techniques described in these recipes will stand you in good stead in other areas of cooking, too. For instance, you may want to poach chicken breasts for cold sliced chicken or cook dried beans for a bean salad. Turn to these pages to learn how.

It may seem unduly complicated in a book about sandwiches to roast a turkey breast or poach salmon fillets. I recognize this, and in an effort to be realistic, I give alternatives to these throughout the book in the sandwich and soup recipes. Deli turkey, canned chicken broth, vegetable bouillon cubes, and canned beans are all acceptable alternatives to these recipes, but for the best health and flavor, I suggest starting from scratch. I understand this is not always possible, but with a little planning it may be more approachable than you think. Stocks can be frozen, as can cooked turkey, chicken, and beans. It takes minutes to poach a salmon fillet and only a little more than that to mix up a batch of granola. When you prepare food yourself you know exactly what you're getting, which means there are no preservatives or additives. That's worth it, don't you agree?

Finally, buy poultry and fish from reputable purveyors. If you can, purchase free-range, organic turkey and chicken and look for the freshest fish in the market. The fish should be firm and glistening and should smell only of the sea, not fishy.

ROAST TURKEY BREAST

Makes about 4 cups cubed turkey or enough slices for 6 to 8 sandwiches

Since there are so many recipes in this book calling for cubed or sliced turkey, I thought it would be helpful to provide a recipe for roasting a whole turkey breast. A two-and-a-half-pound turkey breast provides sufficient meat but certainly not nearly as much as a whole turkey! Good news for everyone with small families. Plus, white turkey meat (breast meat) is very low in fat and calories while still being a good source of protein, niacin, and vitamin B_6. For example, a three-ounce serving of skinned breast meat has about 120 calories and less than two grams of fat, while the same amount of dark meat has 145 calories and as much as five grams of fat.

continued

You may, in the interest of time, choose to buy cooked turkey meat for some of the recipes, but if you can, consider roasting a breast. It will taste better and cost less. Leftover cooked turkey can be frozen for as long as a month. Once it's cool, wrap it well in plastic and foil, and stow it in the freezer. It's handy to have on hand. And finally, save the bones to make the Turkey-Rice Soup on page 156.

1 2½-pound turkey breast half, bone in, skin on
2 teaspoons vegetable oil
Fine sea salt
Freshly ground black pepper
½ cup water

Preheat the oven to 350°F.

Put the turkey breast on a rimmed baking dish or in a shallow 11-by-7-inch roasting pan. Brush with oil and sprinkle with salt and pepper to taste. Pour the water into the pan.

Roast for 20 to 25 minutes per pound, about 1 hour and 25 minutes total. A meat thermometer inserted in the thickest part of the breast will read 165°F. when the meat is done. The juices will run clear yellow when the meat is pierced with a knife.

Let the turkey cool and then remove the skin and cut the meat from the bone. (This is easiest to do when the turkey is slightly warm.) Either slice the meat for sandwiches or cut it into ¾-inch cubes.

HICKORY AND APPLE
SMOKED TURKEY

Makes about 4 cups cubed turkey or enough slices for 6 to 8 sandwiches

I love the flavor of smoked turkey! Smoking it myself gives me control over nitrates and other preservatives that I most certainly do not want in my food, while permitting me to choose my own flavors, such as I have here for Hickory and Apple Smoked Turkey.

Smoking requires no special equipment beyond a covered kettle grill, but it does take a little more time and diligence than roasting a turkey breast in the oven. The water-soaked chips provide smoke and flavor, and are tossed on the fire every half-hour; fresh hot coals need to be added, too, to keep the heat constant. The coals should be covered with ash, not glowing red hot. I pour apple juice in a heatproof pan that is set directly beneath the turkey as it cooks so that as the juice evaporates it infuses the meat with a lovely flavor. While any sturdy pan will do, I often use a secondhand or garage sale baking pan— which I use over and over! Finally, keep in mind that smoking turkey this way gives the meat wonderful flavor but does not extend its keeping qualities. Treat it as you would any roast turkey, storing it in the refrigerator for only a few days and freezing it for longer storage.

continued

4 handfuls of hickory, apple, or pecan wood chips
2 cups natural, unsweetened apple juice
1 2½-pound turkey breast half, bone in, skin on
½ teaspoon fine sea salt
¼ teaspoon finely ground pepper

Soak the wood chips in cold water to cover for at least 30 minutes. Build a charcoal fire on one side of the bottom of a kettle grill with a lid. Use about 20 briquettes. Set a heatproof pan on the other side of the grill, next to the briquettes. Pour the apple juice into the pan.

Sprinkle the turkey breast with salt and pepper. When the fire is medium-hot and gray ash covers the coals, set the turkey on the grid above the heatproof pan. Insert a meat thermometer into the thickest part of the breast. Scoop a handful of wood chips from the water and carefully sprinkle them over the hot coals.

Pile more coals in a small hibachi or charcoal chimney. Light them so that they are glowing and ready to add to the fire every 30 minutes.

Cover the grill and cook the turkey for 30 minutes to the pound, about 2 hours total. The meat thermometer will read 165°F. Add fresh, hot coals to the fire every 30 minutes and toss more wood chips on the coals.

Let the turkey stand for at least 10 minutes. Remove the skin and cut the meat from the bone. (This is easiest to do when the turkey is slightly warm.) Either slice the meat for sandwiches or cut it into ¾-inch cubes.

POACHED CHICKEN BREAST

Makes about 3 cups cubed chicken or enough slices for 3 to 4 sandwiches

Poaching chicken breasts is the classic preparation if you are planning to serve the chicken cold. The gentle cooking method leaves the meat moist and plump. Here I poach a whole breast, which with chicken is generally sold in two pieces. Reserve the flavorful poaching broth for adding to soups. (It can be refrigerated for three days and frozen for up to two months.) Like turkey, cooked and cooled chicken meat can be frozen for as long as a month without loosing flavor. Wrap it well in plastic and foil.

2 chicken breast halves (about 12 ounces total), bone in, skin on
1 small onion, unpeeled, chopped
1 small carrot, chopped
1 small celery rib, chopped
2 sprigs fresh parsley
6 peppercorns
⅛ teaspoon dried thyme
½ bay leaf

Spray a heavy saucepan with nonstick cooking spray. Heat a heavy saucepan over medium-high heat until hot. Cook the chicken breasts, skin side down, in the hot pan for about 4 minutes or until the skin browns. Transfer the breasts to a plate.

Put the onion, carrot, and celery into the hot pan. Cover and cook over medium heat for about 5 minutes, stirring occasionally, or until the vegetables are softened.

Return the chicken breasts to the saucepan and add just enough water to cover them. Bring to a simmer and skim off any foam. Add the parsley, peppercorns, thyme, and bay leaf. Simmer, uncovered, for about 20 minutes. Remove the pan from the heat, cover, and let sit for 30 minutes. Remove the breasts and let them cool completely. Strain the broth for another use, discarding the vegetables.

When the chicken is cool, remove the skin and cut the meat from the bone. Either slice the meat for sandwiches or cut it into ¾-inch cubes.

POACHED SALMON FILLETS

Makes about 2 cups flaked, cooked salmon

Nothing surpasses the flavor and texture of fresh fish, which is why I include an easy recipe for poaching salmon fillets. Use these in place of canned salmon in any recipe. Poaching is a simple and speedy procedure.

2 cups water
1 medium onion, sliced
1 celery rib with leaves, chopped
2 sprigs fresh parsley
1/8 teaspoon dried thyme
1/4 teaspoon fine sea salt
4 peppercorns
2 8-ounce salmon fillets, skin on

In a medium skillet, bring the water, onion, celery, parsley, thyme, salt, and peppercorns to a boil over medium heat. Reduce the heat to low and simmer for 5 minutes.

Lay the salmon fillets in the poaching liquid. Cover the pan and simmer for about 8 minutes or until the salmon flakes with a fork. Using a slotted spatula, transfer the salmon to a plate to cool completely. Remove the skin and then flake the salmon with a fork.

CHICKEN STOCK

Makes about 2 quarts (8 cups)

I think you will agree that after bread baking, making stock is one of the more satisfying kitchen tasks. And the bonus is that once done, you have a refrigerator or freezer filled with stock waiting to be used in nourishing soups when the mood strikes. I understand that there are times when canned chicken broth or a bouillon cube is necessary (we're not always well organized!), but please use the low-sodium varieties sold in most supermarkets and in natural foods stores.

To ensure that the stock is as fat-free as possible, refrigerate the cooled strained broth overnight and then skim the fat that solidifies on the surface.

3   pounds chicken backs, necks, or wings, or a combination, rinsed and
       patted dry
1   large onion, unpeeled and chopped
1   medium carrot, chopped
1   celery rib with leaves, chopped
3   quarts (12 cups) cold water
2   sprigs fresh parsley
½   teaspoon dried thyme
1   bay leaf
½   teaspoon fine sea salt
8   peppercorns

Spray a large soup pot with nonstick cooking spray. Set over medium-high heat and cook the chicken parts, skin side down, for about 8 minutes, turning once, until browned on both sides. Add the onion, carrot, and celery, cover, and cook for about 5 minutes or until the vegetables soften. Add the water and bring to a boil over high heat.

Skim the foam that rises to the surface. Add the parsley, thyme, bay leaf, salt, and peppercorns. Reduce the heat to low and simmer, uncovered, for 3 hours.

Let the stock stand off the heat for 5 minutes and then skim any yellow fat from the surface. Strain the stock into a large bowl and discard the solids. Use immediately or let it cool and refrigerate it for up to 2 days in a covered container, or freeze for up to 3 months.

VEGETABLE STOCK
Makes about 2 quarts (8 cups)

I am happy to report that Americans have embraced vegetable stock to the extent that I have seen canned broth in supermarkets next to chicken and beef broth. Natural foods stores stock it, too, and also sell low-sodium bouillon cubes, which are fine to use in a pinch. But I find vegetable stock so easy to make, I rarely resort to these commercial solutions. Almost any combination of vegetables works, and the following formula produces a tasty brew just right for any number of soups.

2½ quarts (10 cups) cold water
1 large onion, unpeeled and chopped
2 medium carrots, chopped
2 celery ribs with leaves, chopped
2 large baking potatoes, unpeeled, scrubbed, and quartered
2 medium tomatoes, chopped
2 garlic cloves, unpeeled and crushed
½ teaspoon dried thyme
1 bay leaf
½ teaspoon fine sea salt
8 peppercorns

In a large soup pot, combine all the ingredients. Bring to a boil over high heat. Reduce the heat to low and simmer, partially covered, for 3 hours. Strain the stock into a large bowl and discard the solids. Use immediately or let it cool and refrigerate it for up to 3 days in a covered container, or freeze for up to 3 months.

COOKED BEANS

Makes about 5 cups

Cooking dried beans is a simple but time-consuming task. The beans must be soaked before cooking (split peas and lentils are exceptions) for at least six hours, although, depending on the age of the beans, longer soaking may make them more digestible. Their digestibility is greatly enhanced, too, by changing the soaking water several times during soaking. Soaked beans must be cooked very gently until fork-tender, or until you can mash one easily against the roof of your mouth without the bean completely losing its shape. If time is an issue, quick soaking is an acceptable method (see below). Cooked beans can be frozen in a tightly lidded container or a freezer-safe sealable plastic bag for up to 1 month.

There are many different colors, sizes, and shapes of dried beans, so you have to be a little flexible when cooking them. The volume of dried beans varies slightly with type, but generally, one pound measures 2 to 2½ cups, and will yield double its volume when cooked. In other words, 8 ounces (1 cup to 1¼ cups) dried beans will give you about 2 cups cooked. One sixteen-ounce can will yield about 1 cup drained beans.

2½ cups (about 1 pound) dried beans, such as kidney, navy, black, or
      adzuki

continued

Rinse the beans, picking them over to remove any broken pieces. Drain the beans and put them in a large pot. Add enough cold water to cover by at least 2 inches. Soak the beans for 6 hours or overnight in a cool place. Do not refrigerate. If possible, change the water 2 or 3 times during this time.

Drain and rinse the beans. Return them to the pot and cover with fresh water by 2 inches. Bring to a boil over high heat. Skim any foam that rises to the surface. Reduce the heat to medium-low, partly cover, and gently simmer the beans for 45 to 90 minutes or until tender. Drain if necessary and proceed with the specific recipe.

Quick soaking: Put the rinsed, dried beans in a large pot. Cover with water by at least 2 inches and bring to a boil. Boil for 5 to 6 minutes. Remove the pot from the heat, cover, and let the beans sit in the cooking water for 1 hour. Drain the beans and cook them as instructed above.

GRANOLA
Makes about 1 gallon

A handful of crunchy, sweet granola is one of the best revitalizing snacks I know. I have it on hand to use in other recipes and to eat just as is, taking it along on hikes through the Montana mountains, and on camping and road trips. My boys eat it for breakfast, either dry or with a little skim milk and fresh fruit. Granola keeps well in a tightly covered jar or canister, and while it requires an hour in the oven, it's easy to prepare. The nuts and oil provide essential fatty acids and vitamins, which are a trade-off for the relatively high calorie and fat contents. Add the coconut and lemon zest for fuller flavor.

1¼ cups honey
⅔ cup cold water
⅓ cup canola or safflower oil
½ cup powdered whey
½ cup sesame seeds
1 tablespoon ground cinnamon
2 teaspoons grated lemon zest (optional)
1½ teaspoons fine sea salt
10 cups old-fashioned rolled oats
1 cup raw sunflower seeds
1 cup wheat germ
1 cup unsweetened shredded coconut (optional)
½ cup wheat bran
1 cup sliced almonds
1 cup raisins

continued

Preheat the oven to 225°F.

In a medium bowl, whisk together the honey, water, oil, whey, sesame seeds, cinnamon, lemon zest if desired, and salt.

In a larger bowl, stir together the oats, sunflower seeds, wheat germ, coconut if desired, wheat bran, and almonds. Add the honey and water mixture and mix well.

Spread the granola evenly on 2 baking sheets or jelly-roll pans. Bake for 1 hour, stirring carefully every 15 minutes. Halfway through baking, switch the position of the baking sheets.

Take the granola from the oven and let it cool completely on the baking sheets. When cool, toss with the raisins. Store at room temperature in a tightly lidded container.

CHAPTER
—·—9—·—

Soups and Stews

I'm sure you agree with me that a book about sandwiches is not complete without a section on soups and stews. Soup and a sandwich is a classic American team. I also think a book that includes as many recipes as this one does for homemade breads deserves recipes for dishes that cry out for bread accompaniments. I like to serve Flax and Honey Bread (page 205) or 100 Percent Whole Wheat Bread (page 199) with Scandinavian Split Pea Soup and Russian Black Bread (page 217) with Borscht.

Soups and stews are warming, nourishing, and easy to make well ahead of time, which designates them for the kind of cooking I espouse. They are also chock-full of vegetables, grains, and potatoes—foods everyone loves and of which we all need to eat more.

You can never go wrong setting a tureen of soup or pot of stew on the table along with wholesome sandwiches or slices of homemade bread. These are simple and hearty family meals destined to be among everyone's favorites.

TOMATO SOUP

Serves 6 to 8

Most people know tomato soup as coming from a can. This is a shame, since it's a bird of a different feather when homemade with ripe, juicy plum tomatoes. I specify plum tomatoes because they tend to be the most consistently fresh tomatoes available year-round, but feel free to use any ripe red tomatoes. If you have your own garden patch or last summer's put-ups, all the better! I suggest cubes of day-old bread in the soup as a way to make the meal more substantial and also as a tasty way to use up leftover bread.

As a note of interest, in Italy they make a similar soup called *zuppa di pomodoro*. To make the thick, nourishing brew, stir four cups of bread cubes into the following soup after it has cooked for an hour. Let the soup simmer for another 15 minutes or so, stirring it often until it is quite thick. While Basic White Bread (page 184) or 100 Percent Whole Wheat Bread (page 199) does well in this soup, for a change of pace try Spelt Bread (page 226) or French Wheat Hoagies (page 186).

2 tablespoons extra-virgin olive oil
2 medium onions, chopped
2 garlic cloves, minced
6 cups seeded and chopped ripe plum tomatoes; or 3 28-ounce cans low-
     sodium tomatoes, drained and chopped
4 cups Chicken Stock (page 140) or low-sodium canned chicken broth
1 teaspoon fine sea salt
½ teaspoon paprika, preferably Hungarian sweet
3 tablespoons chopped fresh basil, or 2 teaspoons dried
Dash of cayenne pepper
1 cup day-old bread, cut into 1-inch cubes (optional)
Chopped fresh basil, for garnish

In a large soup pot, heat the oil over medium heat. Add the onions and garlic, cover, and cook for about 5 minutes or until vegetables are softened, but not brown, about 5 minutes. Stir in the remaining ingredients except the bread cubes and garnish.

   Bring to a simmer and cook over low heat for about 1 hour. Serve hot, garnished with bread cubes, if desired, and basil.

BROCCOLI BISQUE

Serves 6 to 8

No doubt about it. Broccoli is one of the best buys, healthwise, in the super-market. It's also inexpensive and plentiful nearly all year long. A rich source of valuable beta-carotene, as well as vitamins C and B_1 and calcium, it's a powerhouse of nutrition. And when cooked into a thick, creamlike bisque, it quickly becomes a soup fancy enough to serve company.

1 bunch fresh broccoli, cut into florets, stems reserved
1 tablespoon canola oil
1 medium onion, chopped
1 medium carrot, chopped
1 celery rib, finely chopped
2 garlic cloves, pressed or minced
1 large baking potato, peeled and cut into ¾-inch cubes
6 cups Chicken Stock (page 140) or Vegetable Stock (page 142)
1 teaspoon salt-free herb and spice blend
1 teaspoon fine sea salt
Freshly ground pepper
1 cup low-fat milk (1 percent)

Cut the broccoli stems crosswise into 1-inch pieces.

In a large soup pot, heat the oil over medium heat. Add the onion, carrot, celery, and garlic, and cook for about 5 minutes, covered, or until the vegetables are softened but not brown. Add the broccoli florets and stems, potato, stock, herb and spice blend, salt, and pepper to taste. Bring to a simmer, reduce the heat to low, and cook for 15 to 20 minutes, partly covered, or until the vegetables are tender.

Using a slotted spoon, transfer about half the vegetables to a food processor or blender and puree. If using a blender, you may have to do this in batches. Stir the pureed vegetables into the soup and add the milk. Heat over medium heat until hot, but not boiling.

PAPA'S GARLIC-POTATO SOUP

Serves 8 to 10

My dad likes to make a soup very similar to this one. It's a bold flavored and textured soup thickened with mashed potatoes. Mild leeks lend a satisfying depth of flavor to dishes, but take care to rinse them well under cold running water to rid them of sand. Another good way to get rid of the gritty sand is to nick the root end and soak the leeks in a sinkful of cold water for ten or fifteen minutes.

continued

1 tablespoon canola oil
1 medium onion, chopped
1 medium leek, white part only, chopped
2 celery ribs, chopped
6 large baking potatoes, peeled and cut into 1-inch pieces
6 cups Chicken Stock (page 140), Vegetable Stock (page 142), or low-
    sodium chicken or vegetable broth, or water
6 garlic cloves, minced
1 teaspoon fine sea salt
Freshly ground pepper
2 cups low-fat milk (1 percent)
3 tablespoons chopped fresh chives or parsley

In a large soup pot, heat the oil over medium heat. Add the onion, leek, and celery. Cover and cook for about 5 minutes or until the vegetables are softened but not brown. Add the potatoes, stock, garlic, salt, and pepper. Bring to a simmer. Cover and cook for about 20 minutes or until the potatoes are tender.

Lift the potatoes from the pot with a slotted spoon and mash them until smooth with a potato masher or fork. Stir the mashed potatoes into the soup and add the milk. Heat over medium heat until hot but not boiling. Sprinkle with chives or parsley and serve.

GAZPACHO

Serves 8 to 10

This no-cook vegetable soup is one of the best things about summer, especially if you have tomatoes, peppers, and cucumbers from your own or a neighbor's garden. I suggest buying a multivegetable juice from the health food store that's low in sodium and high in flavor and is mainly tomato juice. If you own a juicer, make your own veggie juice, relying on tomatoes and cucumbers as the base.

1 small onion, quartered
4 beefsteak tomatoes, quartered; or 10 plum tomatoes, sliced
1 green bell pepper, seeded and quartered
1 medium cucumber, peeled and cut into 1-inch pieces
2 scallions, chopped
2 garlic cloves, finely chopped
2 tablespoons fresh lemon juice
4 cups multivegetable tomato juice, chilled
1 teaspoon fine sea salt
Dash of cayenne pepper
1 avocado, pitted, peeled, and finely chopped, for garnish
Crispy Croutons (page 131), for garnish
3 tablespoons chopped fresh parsley, for garnish

continued

In a food processor, pulse the onion, tomatoes, green pepper, cucumber, scallions, and garlic in batches until coarsely chopped. Alternatively, chop the vegetables into ½-inch pieces by hand.

Put the vegetables in a large bowl and stir in the lemon juice, vegetable juice, salt, and cayenne.

Cover and refrigerate at least 2 hours until well chilled. Serve cold with all or one of the garnishes.

SCANDINAVIAN SPLIT PEA SOUP

Serves 6 to 10

Split pea soup is a classic warmer-upper. And when the winter winds blow through our Montana valley, I often make a big pot of this soup to have for lunch or supper with some fresh, sliced 100 Percent Whole Wheat Bread (page 199) or Flax and Honey Bread (page 206). I suggest adding the sliced franks to the soup to make it heartier, but they are not necessary for a great meal. Split peas are dried legumes that, like lentils, do not require soaking before cooking.

5 cups water or Chicken Stock (page 140), Vegetable Stock (page 142),
   or low-sodium chicken or vegetable broth
2½ cups dried yellow split peas (about 1 pound)
2 celery ribs, sliced
1 large onion, chopped
2 medium carrots, sliced
1 teaspoon fine sea salt
½ teaspoon dried thyme
1 tablespoon chopped fresh dill, or 1 teaspoon dried dillweed
⅛ teaspoon grated nutmeg
⅛ teaspoon freshly ground pepper
3 to 4 turkey or vegetarian franks, thinly sliced (optional)
Chopped scallions, for garnish
Crispy Croutons (page 131), for garnish

In a large soup pot, combine the water or stock, split peas, celery, onion, and carrots. Bring to a boil over high heat, reduce the heat to medium, and cook, partly covered, for 1 hour or until the peas are tender. Spoon the peas and vegetables as well as a little liquid into a food processor fitted with the metal blade or a blender and puree. If using a blender, do this in batches. Return pureed vegetables to soup pot.

Season with salt, thyme, dill, nutmeg, and pepper, and if desired, add the sliced franks. Simmer for 10 minutes. Serve hot, garnished with scallions and croutons.

TURKEY-RICE SOUP

Serves 6 to 8

I highly recommend using brown rice in this soup and in general cooking, too. It is not stripped of its nutrient-rich outer layer and consequently is much better for you and your family than white rice. Brown rice takes longer to cook than white rice, but its nutty flavor is well worth the time. I like it in turkey soup, made from the carcass of a roasted turkey breast. The soup is even better made from a smoked turkey carcass.

1 carcass from Roast Turkey Breast (page 133)
6 cups water
4 cups Chicken Stock (page 140), or low-sodium chicken broth
1 medium onion, chopped
2 medium carrots, chopped
2 celery ribs, chopped
¼ cup chopped fresh parsley
1 teaspoon salt-free herb and spice blend
1 bay leaf
½ teaspoon fine sea salt
Freshly ground pepper
½ cup brown rice

In a large soup pot, bring the turkey carcass, water, stock, onion, carrots, and celery to a simmer over medium heat, skimming off any foam that rises to the surface. Add the parsley and herb and spice blend, bay leaf, salt, and pepper to taste. Reduce the heat to low and simmer, partly covered, for 1 hour.

Strain the soup through a large sieve and discard the vegetables or use them in the Garden O' Plenty Bread (page 223). Return the broth to the pot. If desired, reserve the bones and when cool enough to handle, remove any meat clinging to them. Chop the meat and set aside. Discard the bones.

Add the brown rice to the soup broth and cook over medium heat for about 1 hour or until the rice is tender. Stir the chopped turkey meat, if desired, into the soup and serve hot.

HOMEMADE CHICKEN NOODLE SOUP

Serves 6 to 8

When I make chicken noodle soup I rely on the dark meat (chicken thighs) for the most succulent flavor. I use the backs for extra flavor, but discard them entirely before serving the soup. The soup also has a good measure of noodles to keep my children and *me* very happy.

continued

2 pounds chicken thighs
2 pounds chicken backs
1 large onion, chopped
2 medium carrots, chopped
2 celery ribs, sliced
10 cups water
½ teaspoon dried thyme
½ teaspoon dried marjoram
1 bay leaf
¼ cup chopped fresh parsley
Fine sea salt
Freshly ground pepper
4 ounces whole-grain noodles
1 cup fresh green beans, cut into ¾-inch pieces

Spray a large pot with nonstick cooking spray. Lay the chicken thighs skin side down in the pot and cook over medium heat for about 5 minutes or until the skin browns. Turn and cook for another 5 minutes or until the chicken browns on the other side. Transfer the thighs to a plate. Repeat the procedure with the backs and transfer them to the same plate. Pour off all but 1 tablespoon of the chicken fat from the soup pot.

Add the onion, carrots, and celery to the pot. Cover and cook for about 5 minutes or until the vegetables soften. Return the chicken to the pot and add the water. Bring to a boil over high heat, skimming off any foam. Reduce the heat to low and add the thyme, marjoram, bay leaf, parsley, and salt and pepper to taste. Simmer for about 45 minutes or until the chicken is tender. Using tongs, remove the thighs from the soup and set aside to cool. Keep the backs simmering for another 30 minutes.

When cool enough to handle, discard the skin from the thighs, cut the meat from the bones and coarsely chop it.

Remove the soup from the heat and let stand for 5 minutes. Lift the chicken backs from the soup and discard. Skim the fat from the surface. Return the soup to the heat and bring to a simmer. Stir in the chopped meat, noodles, and green beans and cook for about 8 minutes or until the noodles are tender. Adjust the seasoning, if necessary; discard the bay leaf, and serve the soup hot.

SOUTH-OF-THE-BORDER BEAN SOUP

Serves 10 to 12

I prefer this soup, bursting with the sunny flavors of Mexico, made with black beans, but it's good also with kidney or navy (white) beans. Use canned beans if you find it easier, although once you master cooking dried beans, you will discover how easy and economical it is—plus there's the added benefit of no more heavy cans to lug home from the market.

continued

1   tablespoon canola oil
1   large onion, chopped
2   celery ribs, finely chopped
1   large carrot, chopped
2   jalapeño chiles, seeded and finely chopped
1   garlic clove, minced or pressed
6¼ cups cooked black, kidney, or navy beans (see page 143 for
       instructions for cooking beans), or drained canned beans
1   large potato, peeled and shredded
8   cups Chicken Stock (page 140), Vegetable Stock (page 142), or low-
       sodium chicken or vegetable broth, or water
1   teaspoon salt-free herb and spice blend
1   15-ounce can low-sodium tomatoes, undrained
2   tablespoons fresh lemon juice
1   teaspoon fine sea salt
Lemon slices, for garnish
Chopped fresh cilantro, for garnish

In a large soup pot, heat the oil over medium heat. Add the onion, celery, carrot, jalapeño, and garlic. Cover and cook for about 6 minutes or until the vegetables are softened but not brown. Add the beans, potato, stock, and herb and spice blend. Bring to a simmer, and cook for 30 to 60 minutes, covered, or until the beans are just tender.

Stir in the tomatoes and their juice, lemon juice, and salt. Simmer for 20 minutes, or until the beans are quite soft.

Transfer 4 cups of the solids (with a little broth) to a food processor or blender and process until smooth. Return to the pot and heat just until hot. Serve garnished with a lemon slice and cilantro.

CHUCKWAGON SOUP

8 to 10 servings

I call this "chuckwagon" soup to evoke the flavor of the West, where food tends to be hearty and straightforward. The soup is made all in one pot and requires a relatively short cooking time. I add barley because it is rich in niacin, folic acid, and calcium and because it provides the vegetable soup with bulk and great flavor.

1 tablespoon olive oil
1 large onion, chopped
2 celery ribs, chopped
3 medium carrots, chopped
2 garlic cloves, finely chopped
8 cups Chicken Stock (page 140), Vegetable Stock (page 142), or low-sodium chicken or vegetable broth, or water
3 ripe tomatoes, seeded and chopped
½ cup (8-ounce can) low-sodium tomato sauce
½ cup hulled or hulless whole barley
2 teaspoons fine sea salt
¼ cup chopped fresh parsley
1 teaspoon dried oregano
½ teaspoon dried thyme
⅛ teaspoon cayenne pepper
2 cups broccoli florets
1 cup sliced fresh mushrooms

continued

In a large soup pot, heat the oil. Add the onion, celery, carrots, and garlic. Cover and cook for about 5 minutes or until vegetables are softened but not brown. Stir in the stock, tomatoes, tomato sauce, barley, salt, parsley, oregano, thyme, and cayenne. Stir in the broccoli and mushrooms. Cook for about 20 minutes, uncovered, until the barley is tender. Serve hot.

FRESH FRUIT SOUP

Serves 4

Fruit soup may seem like a strange concoction to the uninitiated, but once you try it, you'll make it time and again. I think it's especially good whipped up and eaten right away on a hot summer afternoon or evening. It's also good as a breakfast drink (add a generous tablespoon of plain nonfat yogurt to the processor or blender) or as dessert. It's vital that the banana be frozen, and it helps if the rest of the fruit is chilled, too, as the soup's color will dull if the soup is not served immediately.

2 large bananas
1½ cups unsweetened apple or other fruit juice, chilled
1 large apple, peeled, cored, and chopped
1 large peach, peeled, pitted, and chopped
1 tablespoon fresh lemon juice
1 tablespoon honey
¼ teaspoon ground cinnamon
4 strawberries, sliced
Mint leaves, for garnish

Put the unpeeled bananas in the freezer. Freeze for at least 2 hours until solid. Peel the bananas and cut them into chunks.

In a blender or food processor, puree the frozen bananas with the apple juice, apple, peach, lemon juice, honey, and cinnamon. Transfer to a bowl and stir in the strawberries. Garnish with mint leaves and serve cold.

BORSCHT

Serves 8 to 10

This is one of those all-time great soups that transcends time and cultures. And it's just as delicious served cold as hot. Beets are delicious, full of minerals, particularly iron and calcium, and are also good sources of beta-carotene and vitamin C. Scrub the beets well before shredding them. Serve the soup with Russian Black Bread (page 217).

continued

2 tablespoons canola oil
4 cups shredded green cabbage (about ½ head)
1 medium onion, chopped
1 medium carrot, chopped
1 celery rib, chopped
2 garlic cloves, minced
5 cups Vegetable Stock (page 142), low-sodium vegetable broth, or water
1 cup orange juice
2 cups low-sodium tomato juice
3 tablespoons fresh lemon juice
4 cups shredded beets (about 3 large beets)
2 tablespoons honey
2 teaspoons dried dillweed
½ teaspoon fine sea salt
Freshly ground pepper
½ cup plain nonfat yogurt

In a large soup pot, heat the oil over medium heat. Add the cabbage, onion, carrot, celery, and garlic. Cover and cook for about 10 minutes or until the vegetables are softened. Stir in the stock, orange juice, tomato juice, lemon juice, beets, honey, dill, salt, and pepper to taste. Bring to a simmer over medium heat. Reduce heat to low and cook for about 20 minutes, covered, until the vegetables are tender. Serve hot or chilled with a dollop of yogurt.

MOUNTAIN-MAN CHILI

Serves 6 to 8

Living in the heart of the West, as I do in Montana, I'm used to filling, simple food served in generous portions often from a single pot. Chili fits this description to a tee, and although this version contains no red meat, it's as full-bodied and flavorful as the hardest-riding cowboy or burliest lumberjack could want.

1 tablespoon olive oil
2 medium onions, chopped
1 green bell pepper, seeded and chopped
1 jalapeño chile, seeded and minced; or 1 4-ounce can chopped green
      chiles
2 garlic cloves, minced
1¼ pounds ground turkey
3 tablespoons chili powder
2 teaspoons dried oregano
1 teaspoon fine sea salt
½ teaspoon ground cumin
2 cups cooked red or pinto beans (see page 143 for instructions for
      cooking beans) or drained canned beans
1 28-ounce can low-sodium tomatoes, undrained
Plain nonfat yogurt (optional)
Chopped scallions (optional)
Low-fat cheddar cheese (optional)

continued

In a large soup pot, heat the oil over medium heat. Add the onions, bell pepper, jalapeño, garlic, and turkey, and cook for about 5 minutes, stirring often, or until the turkey loses its pink color. Add the chili powder, oregano, salt, and cumin, and cook for 1 minute, stirring.

Stir in the beans and tomatoes and their liquid, breaking up the tomatoes with a spoon. Bring to a boil, reduce the heat to low, and simmer for about 1 hour, partly covered, until thickened. Ladle the chili into shallow bowls and garnish, if desired, with yogurt, scallions, or cheese.

CHAPTER
—·—10—··—

Desserts and Sweet,
Healthful Snacks

No meal is *really* complete without dessert—not even a simple repast of sandwiches and soup. Desserts do not need to be fancy or oozing with cream and butter to be good. In fact, I prefer light desserts and think that many of us who try to eat healthfully and sensibly are more satisfied with a serving of apple crisp than we are with a gloppy, gooey ice cream sundae.

The following recipes can be served for dessert or as a sweet snack. As much as I deplore the overconsumption of refined white sugar in this country, I understand the craving for sweet foods. I rely on honey, raw sugar, and the natural sweetness of fruit in these desserts. I also depend heavily on whole wheat pastry flour, which is lighter than regular whole wheat flour and therefore works better in cakes and cookies. If your supermarket does not supply it, the natural foods store will.

The next time you are in the mood for something sweet and delicious, whip up a batch of Montana Oatmeal Cookies or a pan of No-Bake Granola Bars. You'll quickly loose any desire for a candy bar or cellophane-wrapped "snack cake." Here is the real thing!

CARROT CAKE WITH NEUFCHÂTEL CHEESE FROSTING

Serves 10 to 12

Carrot cake is a great favorite in my house—as I'm sure it is in yours. This simple version, chock-full of dark raisins and crunchy pecans, bakes in a tube pan in about an hour. I puree the carrots and orange in a blender before adding them to the batter for a super moist, deeply colored cake. If you like frosting (we usually indulge!), coat the cooled cake with this low-fat cream cheese frosting sweetened with honey.

Cake

4 cups whole wheat pastry flour
2 teaspoons baking powder
1 teaspoon baking soda
1½ teaspoons fine sea salt
1 tablespoon ground cinnamon
1 teaspoon grated nutmeg
4 large eggs or 1 cup liquid egg substitute
6 medium carrots, peeled and coarsely chopped (about 12 ounces)
1 large orange, peeled, seeded, and cut into pieces
1 cup (2 sticks) unsalted butter, at room temperature
1 cup honey
2 teaspoons vanilla extract
1 cup chopped pecans
1 cup raisins

Frosting

12 ounces Neufchâtel cheese, at room temperature
½ cup honey
2 teaspoons vanilla extract
2 to 4 tablespoons low-fat or skim milk

To make the cake, preheat the oven to 350°F. Spray a 10-inch tube or bundt pan with nonstick cooking spray or grease and flour the pan. Tap out the excess flour.

In a large bowl, whisk together the flour, baking powder, baking soda, salt, cinnamon, and nutmeg. Set aside.

continued

In a blender set on low, blend the eggs, carrots, and orange for 1 minute to puree. Set aside.

Using an electric mixer set on high, cream the butter and honey for 2 to 3 minutes or beat by hand until light and fluffy. Add the vanilla and blend well.

With the mixer set on medium, alternately add the dry ingredients and egg mixture to the creamed butter and honey. When well mixed, stir in the nuts and raisins by hand.

Scrape the batter into the prepared pan and bake on the middle rack of the oven for 50 minutes to 1 hour, or until lightly browned and the cake begins to pull away from the sides of the pan. Cool the cake for 10 minutes in the pan and then invert it onto a wire rack to cool completely. Frost when cool.

To make the frosting, use an electric mixer set on medium to beat the cheese, honey, and vanilla until smooth. With the mixer running, slowly add enough milk to make a spreadable consistency. Using a metal spatula or kitchen knife, frost the sides and top of the cooled cake.

APPLE CRISP

Serves 8

Apple Crisp has been a Burnett family favorite for more than forty years. My children like it just as much as my sisters and brothers and I did when Mom made it for us with autumn's juiciest apples. It just fills the kitchen with good, comforting smells. If you use powdered tofu milk and butter substitute (a non-margarine butter substitute can be found at natural foods stores), this is a great dairy-free dessert: good news for dessert-lovers with lactose intolerance.

8 medium tart apples (about ¾ pound)
⅓ cup honey
3 tablespoons fresh lemon juice
1½ cups whole wheat pastry flour
½ cup old-fashioned rolled oats
½ cup raw sugar or Sucanat
½ cup powdered whey or powdered milk
1 teaspoon ground cinnamon
½ teaspoon grated nutmeg
¼ teaspoon fine sea salt
½ cup (1 stick) butter, cut into pieces

Preheat the oven to 350°F.

Peel, core, and slice the apples into ¼-inch-thick wedges. Spread in a 9-by-13-inch glass baking dish. Drizzle the honey and lemon juice over the apples.

Combine the flour, oats, sugar, whey, cinnamon, nutmeg, and salt in a large bowl. Add the butter and work with your fingertips or 2 forks until well mixed and crumbly. Sprinkle evenly over the apples.

Bake the crisp for 25 to 30 minutes, or until the apples are tender and the topping is lightly browned.

MONTANA OATMEAL COOKIES

Makes about 7 dozen cookies

These chunky cookies are as big and bold as the Montana sky, filled with hearty, good-for-you ingredients such as oats, nuts, apples, and raisins. I use semisweet (malt-sweetened) carob chips in place of the more traditional chocolate chips. You can buy these tasty morsels in natural foods stores, but be careful you don't mistakenly purchase unsweetened carob chips. They won't taste very appealing in this recipe.

4 cups old-fashioned rolled oats
1 cup chopped walnuts
1 cup unsweetened shredded coconut
1 cup semisweet carob chips
½ cup raisins
1 large, tart apple, peeled, cored, and shredded
½ cup (1 stick) unsalted butter, softened
½ cup almond butter
1½ cups honey
4 large eggs or 1 cup liquid egg substitute
2 teaspoons vanilla extract
Grated zest of 1 large lemon (about 2 teaspoons)
3 cups whole wheat pastry flour
2 teaspoons baking soda
2 teaspoons ground cinnamon

1 **teaspoon grated nutmeg**
1 **teaspoon ground allspice**
1 **teaspoon fine sea salt**

Preheat the oven to 350°F. Spray 2 baking sheets with nonstick cooking spray.

In a large bowl, toss the oats with the walnuts, coconut, carob chips, raisins, and shredded apple. Set aside.

Using an electric mixer set on high, cream the butter, almond butter, and honey for 2 to 3 minutes or beat by hand until fluffy. Add the eggs, vanilla, and lemon zest and beat well.

Whisk together the flour, baking soda, cinnamon, nutmeg, allspice, and salt. Add to the butter mixture and beat just until combined. Stir in the oat mixture.

Drop the batter by heaping tablespoons onto the baking sheets, leaving about 2 inches between each cookie.

Set the sheets on the top and center racks of the oven and bake for about 10 minutes or until lightly browned. Switch the position of the baking sheets halfway through baking for even browning. Watch them carefully to prevent overbaking. Let the cookies cool on the baking sheets for 3 minutes before removing to wire racks to cool completely.

PEANUT BUTTER COOKIES

Makes about 3½ dozen cookies

Be sure to use unsweetened, unsalted peanut butter. I usually buy it in health food stores but some supermarkets carry it, too. For a change, use almond or cashew butter in place of peanut butter. Either way, these soft, chewy cookies are a wholesome addition to the cookie jar.

½ **cup (1 stick) unsalted butter, softened**
1 **cup natural peanut butter**
1¼ **cups honey**
2 **large eggs or** ½ **cup liquid egg substitute**
1 **teaspoon vanilla extract**
4 **cups whole wheat pastry flour**
2 **teaspoons baking soda**
¼ **teaspoon fine sea salt**

Preheat the oven to 350°F.

Using an electric mixer set on high, cream the butter, peanut butter, and honey for 2 to 3 minutes or beat by hand until fluffy. Add the eggs and vanilla and beat well.

Whisk together the flour, baking soda, and salt. Add to the butter mixture and beat just until combined.

Drop the batter by heaping tablespoons onto ungreased baking sheets, leaving about 2 inches between each cookie. Flatten each with a fork dipped in cold water to make a criss-cross pattern.

Set the sheets on the top and center racks of the oven and bake for about 10 minutes or until lightly browned. Switch the position of the baking sheets halfway through baking for even browning. Watch them carefully to prevent overbaking. Let the cookies cool on the baking sheets for 3 minutes before removing to wire racks to cool completely.

NO-BAKE GRANOLA BARS

Makes about one dozen bars

Everybody's granola mixtures are a little different from everyone else's. I love this formula pressed into sticky, crunchy bars that require zero time in the oven. I grab a couple of these for breakfast when I'm on the run, or munch one in mid-afternoon when I crave a sweet pick-me-up. The addition of butter and almond butter may add fat, but they're necessary for binding the other ingredients—not to mention for flavor! For less sweetness, omit the carob chips. But if you include them, be sure they are semisweet chips sweetened with malt.

continued

¾ cup honey
½ cup (1 stick) unsalted butter
½ cup almond butter or natural peanut butter
1 tablespoon vanilla extract
3½ cups quick-cooking oats
½ cup wheat germ
½ cup raw sunflower seeds
½ cup shredded unsweetened coconut
½ cup coarsely chopped walnuts
½ cup semisweet carob chips

Line a 9-by-13-inch pan with foil so that 3 to 4 inches overhang each end. Fold the overhang back onto itself to form sturdy handles on each end. Lightly butter the foil or spray it with nonstick cooking spray containing flour.

Cook the honey, butter, and almond butter in a heavy saucepan until boiling. Boil for 1 minute, stirring constantly. Remove from the heat and add the remaining ingredients except the carob chips.

Scrape the mixture into the lined pan. Sprinkle the carob chips evenly over the top. Let the mixture cool completely. When cool, cut into 2½-by-6-inch bars. Lift the bars from the pan using the foil handles and remove to a plate or cookie jar.

DATE SNACKS

Makes about 2 dozen snack balls

Sticky, seductive dates are intensely sweet and make these little balls of flavor as delicious as any candy bar. I use Granola (page 145) and a handful of carob chips that are gently sweetened with malt. These snacks travel well and so are recommended for lunch boxes, car trips, and family outings.

1 cup packed, pitted dates, coarsely chopped
½ cup raw sunflower seeds
½ cup Granola (page 145)
¼ cup sesame seeds
⅓ cup powdered milk or powdered tofu milk
⅓ cup honey
½ cup semisweet carob chips
½ cup unsweetened shredded coconut

In a food processor fitted with the metal blade, process the dates, sunflower seeds, Granola, and sesame seeds until finely chopped. Do not overprocess.

Pour the mixture into a mixing bowl. Add the powdered milk and honey, and stir with a wooden spoon until well mixed. Add the carob chips and ¼ cup of the coconut. Mix well. Using your fingers, press the mixture into 1-inch balls.

Put the remaining ¼ cup coconut in a shallow bowl or saucer. Roll the balls in the coconut to coat. Store at room temperature in a tightly lidded container.

OATMEAL-RAISIN SNACK CAKE

Serves 12 to 16

Snack cakes are unbeatable to have around the house for simple desserts, lunch box fare, and afternoon treats. This one is chock-full of healthful oats and raisins and topped with a nutty, honey-sweetened glaze. Quick-cooking rolled oats are rolled thinner than old-fashioned rolled oats so that they cook a little faster. Take care not to use instant oats.

Snack Cake
1¼ cups boiling water
1 cup quick-cooking rolled oats
¼ cup canola oil
4 tablespoons (½ stick) unsalted butter, softened
¾ cup honey
½ cup liquid egg substitute or 2 large eggs
1 teaspoon vanilla extract
2 cups whole wheat pastry flour
1 teaspoon baking soda
1 teaspoon ground cinnamon
¾ teaspoon ground nutmeg
½ teaspoon fine sea salt
1 cup raisins

Topping

⅓ cup canola oil
½ cup powdered milk or whey
½ cup honey
2 tablespoons low-fat (1 percent) milk
½ cup chopped walnuts

Preheat the oven to 350°F. Spray a 9-by-13-inch pan with nonstick cooking spray; or lightly grease it.

Place the oats, oil, and butter in a medium bowl. Pour in the water and let stand for 20 minutes. Whisk in the honey, egg substitute, and vanilla.

Whisk together the flour, baking soda, cinnamon, nutmeg, and salt. Add to the oat mixture and stir until smooth. Stir in the raisins.

Scrape the batter into the pan and bake for about 30 minutes or until a toothpick inserted 1 inch from the edges comes out clean.

Meanwhile, make the topping. Whisk together the oil, powdered milk, honey, milk, and nuts. When the cake has baked for about 30 minutes, spread it evenly with the topping and return it to the oven for about 10 minutes longer or until the topping is bubbling.

Let the cake cool in the pan set on wire racks. When completely cool, cut into squares or rectangles and serve.

CHAPTER
–·–11–·–

Traditional Breads

The name of this chapter says it all—sort of. The breads here are made with the ingredients you *expect* to find in a traditional collection of bread recipes. All include all-purpose unbleached white flour, which is mixed in varying amounts with whole wheat flour (except in the case of Basic White Bread). In my last book, I referred to this style of recipe as a "transition" recipe—one that would launch the bread baker on the path to using whole-grain flours without giving up familiar white flour completely.

At the same time, many of the breads here are traditional for other reasons. There's a basic whole wheat and white bread and there is Cinnamon-Raisin Bread. Clearly, these breads are familiar sounding and will be familiar tasting. I have also included two slightly off-beat loaves: Cheddar Cheese and Chive Bread and Lemon Bread, both full of flavor and used throughout the book in a number of sandwiches.

Admittedly, these sorts of breads are expected in a sandwich book. They make incredible sandwiches, not to mention toast and bread crumbs. However, their flavors and wholesomeness are perhaps a little less predictable and undeniably superb.

OLD-FASHIONED WHEAT BREAD

Makes one 1½-pound loaf

This is a great bread, and one you will make time and again as it fills so many everyday needs: sandwiches, toast, bread crumbs, and just plain eating, spread with a little all-fruit jam. I include it in this chapter for traditional breads rather than in the next one for whole wheat breads because the recipe includes unbleached all-purpose flour.

continued

¾ cup (6 fluid ounces) water
1 large egg or ¼ cup liquid egg substitute
3 tablespoons canola oil
2 tablespoons honey
1½ cups (7 ounces) whole wheat flour
1½ cups (7½ ounces) unbleached all-purpose flour
3 tablespoons powdered milk
1½ teaspoons fine sea salt
2¼ teaspoons active dry yeast

Put all the ingredients in the inner pan in the order listed, or in the reverse order if the manual for your machine specifies dry ingredients first and liquids last. Select the Basic Wheat cycle, Light setting (or the equivalent setting for your machine; see chart, pages 14–17). Push Start.

OLD-FASHIONED WHEAT BREAD

Variation for one 1-pound loaf

½ cup (4 fluid ounces) water
1 medium egg or 3 tablespoons liquid egg substitute
2 tablespoons canola oil
1½ tablespoons honey
1 cup (4¾ ounces) whole wheat flour
1 cup (5 ounces) unbleached all-purpose flour
2 tablespoons powdered milk
1 teaspoon fine sea salt
1¾ teaspoons active dry yeast

Put all the ingredients in the inner pan in the order listed, or in the reverse order if the manual for your machine specifies dry ingredients first and liquids last. Select the Basic Wheat cycle, Light setting (or the equivalent setting for your machine; see chart, pages 14–17). Push Start.

BASIC WHITE BREAD

Makes one 1½-pound loaf

This is as wholesome and straightforward as a loaf of white bread can be. Some might call this a bread from the heartland, and the description would be apt. For a more nutritious loaf, substitute ¼ cup whole wheat flour for the same amount of unbleached all-purpose. This results in "almost" white bread.

1 cup plus 2 tablespoons (9 fluid ounces) water
2 tablespoons canola oil
1½ tablespoons honey
3 cups (15 ounces) unbleached all-purpose flour
3 tablespoons powdered milk
1½ teaspoons fine sea salt
2 teaspoons active dry yeast

Put all the ingredients in the inner pan in the order listed, or in the reverse order if the manual for your machine specifies dry ingredients first and liquids last. Select the Basic Wheat cycle, Light setting (or the equivalent setting for your machine; see chart, pages 14–17). Push Start.

BASIC WHITE BREAD

Variation for one 1-pound loaf

¾ cup (6 fluid ounces) water
1½ tablespoons canola oil
1 tablespoon honey
2 cups (10 ounces) unbleached all-purpose flour
2 tablespoons powdered milk
1 teaspoon fine sea salt
1½ teaspoons active dry yeast

Put all the ingredients in the inner pan in the order listed, or in the reverse order if the manual for your machine specifies dry ingredients first and liquids last. Select the Basic Wheat cycle, Light setting (or the equivalent setting for your machine; see chart, pages 14–17). Push Start.

FRENCH WHEAT HOAGIES

Makes 6 hoagies

I call these hoagies because of their elongated shape, which is a handy one for sandwiches. To see what I mean, check out the Grilled Turkey Franks with Barbecued Onions (page 55).

¾ **cup (6 fluid ounces) water**
1 **large egg or ¼ cup liquid egg substitute**
3 **tablespoons canola oil**
1½ **tablespoons honey**
1½ **cups (7 ounces) whole wheat flour**
1½ **cups (7½ ounces) unbleached all-purpose flour**
2 **tablespoons powdered milk**
1½ **teaspoons fine sea salt**
2 **teaspoons active dry yeast**
1 **medium egg white, lightly beaten**
1½ **tablespoons sesame seeds**

Put all the ingredients, except the beaten egg white and sesame seeds, in the inner pan in the order listed, or in the reverse order if the manual for your machine specifies dry ingredients first and liquids last. Select the Dough setting (or the equivalent setting for your machine; see chart, pages 14–17). Push Start. When the machine beeps after 1 hour and 20 minutes, remove the dough. Turn off the machine.

Transfer the dough to a lightly floured work surface. Gently roll and stretch it into a 12-inch rope. Slice the rope into 6 equal pieces and form these into rolls. To do so, put a piece of dough in your cupped palm. Cover the dough with your other, slightly cupped hand. Rotate the top hand and use your fingertips and the heel of the top hand to mold the dough gently into a ball. Repeat with the remaining dough pieces. Let the dough rest for 5 minutes. Then roll each one into a hot dog–roll shape about 5 inches long.

Put the rolls on a lightly greased baking sheet, leaving about 2 inches between them. Brush the tops of the rolls with the beaten egg white and sprinkle with sesame seeds. Cover the rolls with a damp kitchen towel or plastic wrap and let rise for about 45 minutes to 1 hour, or until almost doubled in volume.

Preheat the oven to 400°F. Bake the rolls for 12 to 15 minutes or until lightly browned.

FRENCH WHEAT HOAGIES

Variation for 4 hoagies

½ cup (4 fluid ounces) water
1 medium egg or 3 tablespoons liquid egg substitute
2 tablespoons canola oil
1 tablespoon honey
1 cup (4¾ ounces) whole wheat flour
1 cup (5 ounces) unbleached all-purpose flour
1½ tablespoons powdered milk
1 teaspoon fine sea salt
1½ teaspoons active dry yeast
1 small egg white, lightly beaten
1 tablespoon sesame seeds

Put all the ingredients, except the beaten egg white and sesame seeds, in the inner pan in the order listed, or in the reverse order if the manual for your machine specifies dry ingredients first and liquids last. Select the Dough setting (or the equivalent setting for your machine; see chart, pages 14–17). Push Start. When the machine beeps after 1 hour and 20 minutes, remove the dough. Turn off the machine.

Transfer the dough to a lightly floured work surface. Gently roll and stretch it into an 8-inch rope. Slice the rope into 4 equal pieces and form these into rolls. To do so, put a piece of dough in your cupped palm. Cover the dough with your other, slightly cupped hand. Rotate the top hand and use your fingertips and the heel of the top hand to mold the dough gently into a ball. Repeat with the remaining dough pieces. Let the dough rest for 5 minutes. Then roll each one into a hot dog–roll shape about 5 inches long.

Put the rolls on a lightly greased baking sheet, leaving about 2 inches between them. Brush the tops of the rolls with the beaten egg white and sprinkle with sesame seeds. Cover the rolls with a damp kitchen towel or plastic wrap and let rise for about 45 minutes to 1 hour, or until almost doubled in volume.

Preheat the oven to 400°F. Bake the rolls for 12 to 15 minutes or until lightly browned.

CHEDDAR CHEESE AND CHIVE BREAD

Makes one 1½-pound loaf

This hearty, flavorful bread makes great sandwiches. For instance, I pair it with tuna salad (page 36), and it's great! It would be equally fantastic with sliced garden-grown tomatoes or another vegetable.

⅔ cup (5½ fluid ounces) water
2 tablespoons canola oil
1 tablespoon honey
1 cup (4 ounces) shredded extra-sharp cheddar cheese
2 large eggs or ½ cup liquid egg substitute
1½ cups (7 ounces) whole wheat flour
1½ cups (7½ ounces) unbleached all-purpose flour
¼ cup powdered milk
2 tablespoons dried chives
1½ teaspoons fine sea salt
2 teaspoons active dry yeast

Put all the ingredients in the inner pan in the order listed, or in the reverse order if the manual for your machine specifies dry ingredients first and liquids last. Select the Basic Wheat cycle, Light setting (or the equivalent setting for your machine; see chart, pages 14–17). Push Start.

CHEDDAR CHEESE AND CHIVE BREAD

Variation for one 1-pound loaf

⅓ cup (2¾ fluid ounces) water
1½ tablespoons canola oil
2 teaspoons honey
¾ cup (3 ounces) shredded extra-sharp cheddar cheese
2 medium eggs or ⅓ cup liquid egg substitute
1 cup (4¾ ounces) whole wheat flour
1 cup (5 ounces) unbleached all-purpose flour
3 tablespoons powdered milk
1½ tablespoons dried chives
1 teaspoon fine sea salt
1½ teaspoons active dry yeast

Put all the ingredients in the inner pan in the order listed, or in the reverse order if the manual for your machine specifies dry ingredients first and liquids last. Select the Basic Wheat cycle, Light setting (or the equivalent setting for your machine; see chart, pages 14–17). Push Start.

CINNAMON-RAISIN BREAD

Makes one 1½-pound loaf

This has to be one of the all-time great combinations for bread. We love this toasted on cold mornings and we also use it for lots of sandwiches, such as the Pineapple-Peach-Pecan Sandwich (page 105).

1 cup plus 2 tablespoons (9 fluid ounces) water
2 tablespoons canola oil
2 tablespoons honey
1½ cups (7 ounces) whole wheat flour
1½ cups (7½ ounces) unbleached all-purpose flour
3 tablespoons powdered milk
1 teaspoon ground cinnamon
1½ teaspoons fine sea salt
2 teaspoons active dry yeast
¾ cup (3¾ ounces) raisins

Put all the ingredients except ⅓ cup of the raisins in the inner pan in the order listed, or in the reverse order if the manual for your machine specifies dry ingredients first and liquids last. Select the Fruit and Nut setting (or the equivalent setting for your machine; see chart, pages 14–17). Push Start.

Add the remaining ⅓ cup raisins when the machine beeps, about 12 minutes after starting.

CINNAMON-RAISIN BREAD

Variation for one 1-pound loaf

¾ cup (6 fluid ounces) water
1½ tablespoons canola oil
1½ tablespoons honey
1 cup (4¾ ounces) whole wheat flour
1 cup (5 ounces) unbleached all-purpose flour
2 tablespoons powdered milk
¾ teaspoon ground cinnamon
1 teaspoon fine sea salt
1½ teaspoons active dry yeast
½ cup (2½ ounces) raisins

Put all the ingredients except ¼ cup of the raisins in the inner pan in the order listed, or in the reverse order if the manual for your machine specifies dry ingredients first and liquids last. Select the Fruit and Nut setting (or the equivalent setting for your machine; see chart, pages 14–17). Push Start.

Add the remaining ¼ cup raisins when the machine beeps, about 12 minutes after starting.

LEMON BREAD

Makes one 1½-pound loaf

Lemons sweetened ever so lightly with honey give this bread a delicate flavor that's just right for eating plain with a cup of herbal tea or as a bread in the Apricot-and-Pecan Cream Cheese Sandwich (page 109).

1 cup (8 fluid ounces) water
3 tablespoons canola oil
3 tablespoons honey
Zest of 1½ lemons, grated
1½ cups (7 ounces) whole wheat flour
1½ cups (7½ ounces) unbleached all-purpose flour
3 tablespoons powdered milk
1 teaspoon grated nutmeg
1½ teaspoons fine sea salt
2½ teaspoons active dry yeast
½ cup (2½ ounces) raisins

Put all the ingredients except the raisins in the inner pan in the order listed, or in the reverse order if the manual for your machine specifies dry ingredients first and liquids last. Select the Basic Wheat cycle, Light setting (or the equivalent setting for your machine; see chart, pages 14–17). Push Start.

Add the raisins when the machine beeps, about 12 minutes after starting.

LEMON BREAD

Variation for one 1-pound loaf

¾ cup (6 fluid ounces) water
2 tablespoons canola oil
2 tablespoons honey
Zest of 1 lemon, grated
1 cup (4¾ ounces) whole wheat flour
1 cup (5 ounces) unbleached all-purpose flour
2 tablespoons powdered milk
½ teaspoon grated nutmeg
1 teaspoon fine sea salt
2 teaspoons active dry yeast
⅓ cup (2 ounces) raisins

Put all the ingredients except the raisins in the inner pan in the order listed, or in the reverse order if the manual for your machine specifies dry ingredients first and liquids last. Select the Basic Wheat cycle, Light setting (or the equivalent setting for your machine; see chart, pages 14–17). Push Start.

Add the raisins when the machine beeps, about 12 minutes after starting.

CALZONE DOUGH

Makes six 9-inch rounds

Calzone are sealed rounds of dough stuffed with an assortment of savory fillings. The dough is versatile, light, and soft and bakes to a golden turn. In this book, I use it for Mom's Cabbage Burgers (page 58) and Turkey Sausage, Mushroom, and Italian Cheese Calzones (page 60). This dough is equally good as pizza dough.

1 cup plus 2 tablespoons (9 fluid ounces) water
1 tablespoon extra-virgin olive oil
2 teaspoons honey
1½ cups (7 ounces) whole wheat flour
1½ cups (7½ ounces) unbleached all-purpose flour
1½ teaspoons fine sea salt
2 teaspoons active dry yeast

Put all the ingredients in the inner pan in the order listed, or in the reverse order if the manual for your machine specifies dry ingredients first and liquids last. Select the Dough setting (or the equivalent setting for your machine; see chart, pages 14–17). Push Start. When the machine beeps after 1 hour and 20 minutes, remove the dough.

Divide the dough according to individual recipe instructions.

Variation: To make Dilled Calzone Dough, add 2 teaspoons of dried dillweed to the dough when you add the salt.

CALZONE DOUGH

Variation for four 9-inch rounds

¾ cup (6 fluid ounces) water
2 teaspoons extra-virgin olive oil
1 teaspoon honey
1 cup (4¾ ounces) whole wheat flour
1 cup (5 ounces) unbleached all-purpose flour
1 teaspoon fine sea salt
1½ teaspoons active dry yeast

Put all the ingredients in the inner pan in the order listed, or in the reverse order if the manual for your machine specifies dry ingredients first and liquids last. Select the Dough setting (or the equivalent setting for your machine; see chart, pages 14–17). Push Start. When the machine beeps after 1 hour and 20 minutes, remove the dough.

Divide the dough according to individual recipe instructions.

Variation: To make Dilled Calzone Dough, add 1¼ teaspoons of dried dillweed to the dough when you add the salt.

CHAPTER
–·–12–·–

Whole Wheat and
Rye Breads

If any group of breads is closer to my heart than another, it has to be this one. The recipes in this chapter are shining examples of the way I think bread ought to be. These are full-bodied, boldly flavored, earthy loaves made with whole grains and whole wheat flour. When you think of complex carbohydrates, fiber, and B vitamins, think of these breads. In other words, these breads are very, very good for you. And you don't have to go to a natural foods bakery to enjoy them. You can make them in your bread machine so that they are always on hand.

100 PERCENT WHOLE WHEAT BREAD

Makes one 1½-pound loaf

Here is one of the all-time best breads. Made from whole wheat flour exclusively, it's a perfect sandwich or toasting bread, full of nutrients and fiber. What could be better?

1   cup plus 2 tablespoons (9 fluid ounces) water
1½ tablespoons canola oil
1½ tablespoons honey
½   teaspoon liquid lecithin
3   cups (14 ounces) whole wheat flour
3   tablespoons powdered whey
2   tablespoons gluten flour
1½ teaspoons fine sea salt
2   teaspoons active dry yeast

Put all the ingredients in the inner pan in the order listed, or in the reverse order if the manual for your machine specifies dry ingredients first and liquids last. Select the Basic Wheat cycle, Light setting (or the equivalent setting for your machine; see chart, pages 14–17). Push Start.

100 PERCENT WHOLE WHEAT BREAD

Variation for one 1-pound loaf

¾ cup (6 fluid ounces) water
1 tablespoon canola oil
1 tablespoon honey
¼ teaspoon liquid lecithin
2 cups (9½ ounces) whole wheat flour
2 tablespoons powdered whey
1½ tablespoons gluten flour
1 teaspoon fine sea salt
1½ teaspoons active dry yeast

Put all the ingredients in the inner pan in the order listed, or in the reverse order if the manual for your machine specifies dry ingredients first and liquids last. Select the Basic Wheat cycle, Light setting (or the equivalent setting for your machine; see chart, pages 14–17). Push Start.

MULTIGRAIN BREAD

Makes one 1½-pound loaf

This is one of the most versatile breads in the book. It's a great favorite in the Burnett home, showing up on meal tables at all times of day and in lunch boxes for sandwiches.

1¼ cup (10 fluid ounces) water
½ cup plus 2 tablespoons Multigrain Cereal Mix (page 204)
1½ tablespoons canola oil
1 tablespoon unsulfured molasses
1 teaspoon honey
½ teaspoon liquid lecithin (optional)
3 cups (14 ounces) whole wheat flour
3 tablespoons powdered whey
2 tablespoons gluten flour
1½ teaspoons fine sea salt
2½ teaspoons active dry yeast

Put all the ingredients except 2 tablespoons of Multigrain Cereal Mix in the inner pan in the order listed, or in the reverse order if the manual for your machine specifies dry ingredients first and liquids last. Select the Basic Wheat cycle, Light setting (or the equivalent setting for your machine; see chart, pages 14–17). Push Start.

continued

Watch the time on the bread machine. When there are 1 hour and 34 minutes left in the kneading cycle (or just before the last punch down on machines other than the Breadman), open the lid, use a pastry brush to brush the top of the dough with water. Sprinkle the remaining 2 tablespoons of Multigrain Cereal Mix on the surface of the bread, pressing it lightly so that it adheres. Close the lid and let the machine complete the cycle.

MULTIGRAIN BREAD

Variation for one 1-pound loaf

¾ cup plus 2 tablespoons (7 fluid ounces) water
⅓ cup plus 1½ tablespoons Multigrain Cereal Mix (page 204)
1 tablespoon canola oil
2 teaspoons unsulfured molasses
¾ teaspoon honey
¼ teaspoon liquid lecithin (optional)
2 cups (9½ ounces) whole wheat flour
2 tablespoons powdered whey
1½ tablespoons gluten flour
1 teaspoon fine sea salt
2 teaspoons active dry yeast

Put all the ingredients except 1½ tablespoons of Multigrain Cereal Mix in the inner pan in the order listed, or in the reverse order if the manual for your machine specifies dry ingredients first and liquids last. Select the Basic Wheat cycle, Light setting (or the equivalent setting for your machine; see chart, pages 14–17). Push Start.

Watch the time on the bread machine. When there are 1 hour and 34 minutes left in the kneading cycle (or just before the last punch down on machines other than the Breadman), open the lid and use a pastry brush to brush the top of the dough with water. Sprinkle the remaining 1½ tablespoons of Multigrain Cereal Mix on the surface of the bread, pressing it lightly so that it adheres. Close the lid and let the machine complete the cycle.

- - -·- -·- -·- -·- -·- -·- - -

MULTIGRAIN CEREAL MIX

Makes about 7½ cups

Because Multigrain Bread is one of my favorites, I always keep a stash of this cereal mix on hand so that I can bake this bread anytime the mood strikes. I also eat this cooked like oatmeal and sweetened with honey.

1½ cups rolled wheat, 1½ cups old-fashioned rolled oats, 1½ cups rolled rye, and 1½ cups rolled barley; *or* 6 cups (1 pound) pre-mixed rolled grains
¾ cup raw shelled sunflower seeds
½ cup whole flax seed
¼ cup whole millet

Stir all ingredients together and mix thoroughly. Store in a sealed plastic bag or tightly lidded glass jar.

FLAX AND HONEY BREAD

Makes one 1½-pound loaf

Flaxseed blends well with wheat flour and provides linolenic acid, which has been shown to help prevent some tumors. Both flaxseed and flax oil are sold in natural foods stores.

⅔ cup (4 ounces) flaxseed
1 cup plus 2 tablespoons (9 fluid ounces) water
1½ tablespoons canola oil
1½ tablespoons honey
½ teaspoon liquid lecithin
2½ cups (12 ounces) whole wheat flour
¼ cup sunflower seeds
3 tablespoons powdered whey
2 tablespoons gluten flour
1½ teaspoons fine sea salt
2½ teaspoons active dry yeast

Put flaxseed in a blender and process until finely ground.

Put all the ingredients in the inner pan in the order listed, or in the reverse order if the manual for your machine specifies dry ingredients first and liquids last. Select the Basic Wheat cycle, Light setting (or the equivalent setting for your machine; see chart, pages 14–17). Push Start.

FLAX AND HONEY BREAD

Variation for one 1-pound loaf

½ cup (2¾ ounces) flaxseed
¾ cup (6 fluid ounces) water
1 tablespoon canola oil
1 tablespoon honey
¼ teaspoon liquid lecithin
1¾ cups (8¾ ounces) whole wheat flour
2 tablespoons sunflower seeds
2 tablespoons powdered whey
1½ tablespoons gluten flour
1 teaspoon fine sea salt
2 teaspoons active dry yeast

Put flaxseed in a blender and process until finely ground.

   Put all the ingredients in the inner pan in the order listed, or in the reverse order if the manual for your machine specifies dry ingredients first and liquids last. Select the Basic Wheat cycle, Light setting (or the equivalent setting for your machine; see chart, pages 14–17). Push Start.

OATMEAL SPICE BREAD

Makes one 1½-pound loaf

To make this bread you need cooked and completely cooled oatmeal made from old-fashioned rolled oats. Teaming the oatmeal with whole wheat and oat flour makes this a particularly high-fiber bread. It's great with fruit, as in the Strawberries, Dates, and Almond Butter Sandwich (page 104).

¾ cup (6 fluid ounces) hot tap water
¾ cup (6½ ounces) cold cooked oatmeal
2 tablespoons canola oil
2 tablespoons honey
½ teaspoon liquid lecithin
2½ cups (12 ounces) whole wheat flour
½ cup (2 ounces) oat flour
3 tablespoons powdered whey
1 tablespoon gluten flour
1½ teaspoons fine sea salt
1 teaspoon ground cinnamon
½ teaspoon grated nutmeg
2½ teaspoons active dry yeast
½ cup raisins

continued

Put all the ingredients in the inner pan in the order listed, or in the reverse order if the manual for your machine specifies dry ingredients first and liquids last. Select the Basic Wheat cycle, Light setting (or the equivalent setting for your machine; see chart, pages 14–17). Push Start.

OATMEAL SPICE BREAD

Variation for one 1-pound loaf

½ cup (4 fluid ounces) hot tap water
½ cup (4¼ ounces) cold cooked oatmeal
1½ tablespoons canola oil
1½ tablespoons honey
¼ teaspoon liquid lecithin
1¾ cups (8¾ ounces) whole wheat flour
¼ cup (1½ ounces) oat flour
2 tablespoons powdered whey
2 teaspoons gluten flour
1 teaspoon fine sea salt
½ teaspoon ground cinnamon
¼ teaspoon grated nutmeg
1½ teaspoons active dry yeast
¼ cup raisins

Put all the ingredients in the inner pan in the order listed, or in the reverse order if the manual for your machine specifies dry ingredients first and liquids last. Select the Basic Wheat cycle, Light setting (or the equivalent setting for your machine; see chart, pages 14–17). Push Start.

BANANA-NUT BREAD

Makes one 1½-pound loaf

Bananas and walnuts are a match made in bread heaven. I toss in a handful of pitted dates to expand the celestial arena and also rely on a little walnut oil to round out the flavors. The result? A bread fit for angels—or for pairing with cranberry sauce and oranges, as described on page 106. Imported French walnut oil has the most potent flavor of all walnut oils, but because it's expensive, feel free to use any nut oil or even canola or sesame oil. However, the flavor of the baked loaf won't be quite the same.

¾ cup plus 2 tablespoons (7 fluid ounces) water
2 tablespoons raw sugar
1½ tablespoons walnut oil
2 teaspoons fresh lemon juice
1 teaspoon vanilla extract
½ teaspoon liquid lecithin
½ cup mashed ripe banana
3 cups (14 ounces) whole wheat flour
3 tablespoons powdered whey
2 tablespoons gluten flour
1 teaspoon fine sea salt
2½ teaspoons active dry yeast
⅓ cup (1½ ounces) finely chopped walnuts
⅓ cup (2 ounces) chopped pitted dates

Put all the ingredients, except the walnuts and dates, in the inner pan in the order listed, or in the reverse order if the manual for your machine specifies dry ingredients first and liquids last. Select Fruit and Nut setting (or the equivalent setting for your machine; see chart, pages 14–17). Push Start.

Add the walnuts and dates when machine beeps, about 12 minutes after starting.

BANANA-NUT BREAD

Variation for one 1-pound loaf

⅔ cup (5½ fluid ounces) water
1 tablespoon raw sugar
1 tablespoon walnut oil
1½ teaspoons fresh lemon juice
¾ teaspoon vanilla extract
¼ teaspoon liquid lecithin
⅓ cup mashed ripe banana
2 cups (9½ ounces) whole wheat flour
2 tablespoons powdered whey
1½ tablespoons gluten flour
¾ teaspoon fine sea salt
2 teaspoons active dry yeast
¼ cup (1 ounce) finely chopped walnuts
¼ cup (1½ ounces) chopped pitted dates

Put all the ingredients, except the walnuts and dates, in the inner pan in the order listed, or in the reverse order if the manual for your machine specifies dry ingredients first and liquids last. Select the Fruit and Nut setting (or the equivalent setting for your machine; see chart, pages 14–17). Push Start.

Add the walnuts and dates when machine beeps, about 12 minutes after starting.

CARAWAY RYE BREAD

Makes one 1½-pound loaf

Caraway seeds impart their own special flavor that teams nicely with rye. I like this bread with Grilled Cheese and Tomato (page 76).

1 cup plus 2 tablespoons (9 fluid ounces) water
2 tablespoons canola oil
2 tablespoons unsulfured molasses
½ teaspoon liquid lecithin
2¼ cups (10¾ ounces) whole wheat flour
¾ cup (3½ ounces) rye flour
¼ cup dried minced onion
3 tablespoons powdered whey
2 tablespoons gluten flour
1 tablespoon carob powder
1 tablespoon caraway seeds
1 teaspoon dried dillweed
1½ teaspoons fine sea salt
2½ teaspoons active dry yeast

Put all the ingredients in the inner pan in the order listed, or in the reverse order if the manual for your machine specifies dry ingredients first and liquids last. Select the European setting (or the equivalent setting for your machine; see chart, pages 14–17). Push Start.

CARAWAY RYE BREAD

Variation for one 1-pound loaf

¾ cup (6 fluid ounces) water
1½ tablespoons canola oil
1½ tablespoons unsulfured molasses
¼ teaspoon liquid lecithin
1½ cups (7½ ounces) whole wheat flour
½ cup (2½ ounces) rye flour
3 tablespoons dried minced onion
2 tablespoons powdered whey
1½ tablespoons gluten flour
2 teaspoons carob powder
2 teaspoons caraway seeds
¾ teaspoon dried dillweed
1 teaspoon fine sea salt
2 teaspoons active dry yeast

Put all the ingredients in the inner pan in the order listed, or in the reverse order if the manual for your machine specifies dry ingredients first and liquids last. Select the European setting (or the equivalent setting for your machine; see chart, pages 14–17). Push Start.

PUMPERNICKEL BREAD

Makes one 1½-pound loaf

Pumpernickel bread is nothing more than dark rye bread. The rye flour gives it intense flavor and a pleasingly dense texture. Try it with salmon salad (page 41) or Neufchâtel cheese and chives (page 108).

1¼ cups (10 fluid ounces) water
1 tablespoon canola oil
1 tablespoon unsulfured molasses
½ teaspoon liquid lecithin
2 cups (9½ ounces) whole wheat flour
1 cup (4¾ ounces) rye flour
4 tablespoons powdered whey
3 tablespoons gluten flour
3 tablespoons carob powder
1 tablespoon caraway seeds
1½ teaspoons fine sea salt
2½ teaspoons active dry yeast

Put all the ingredients in the inner pan in the order listed, or in the reverse order if the manual for your machine specifies dry ingredients first and liquids last. Select the European setting (or the equivalent setting for your machine; see chart, pages 14–17). Push Start.

PUMPERNICKEL BREAD

Variation for one 1-pound loaf

¾ cup (6 fluid ounces) water
2 teaspoons canola oil
2 teaspoons unsulfured molasses
¼ teaspoon liquid lecithin
1⅓ cups (6¼ ounces) whole wheat flour
⅔ cup (3¼ ounces) rye flour
3 tablespoons powdered whey
2 tablespoons gluten flour
2 tablespoons carob powder
2 teaspoons caraway seeds
1 teaspoon fine sea salt
2 teaspoons active dry yeast

Put all the ingredients in the inner pan in the order listed, or in the reverse order if the manual for your machine specifies dry ingredients first and liquids last. Select the European setting (or the equivalent setting for your machine; see chart, pages 14–17). Push Start.

RUSSIAN BLACK BREAD

Makes one 1½-pound loaf

Very similar to Pumpernickel Bread (page 215), Russian Black Bread is a full-flavored, dark bread that stands up to strong flavors such as sardines (page 39) and smoked turkey (page 33). The Postum intensifies the flavor of the bread and is sold in natural foods stores and many supermarkets.

1 cup plus 2 tablespoons (9 fluid ounces) water
1 tablespoon canola oil
2 tablespoons unsulfured molasses
1 tablespoon honey
½ teaspoon liquid lecithin
2½ cups (12 ounces) whole wheat flour
½ cup (2 ounces) rye flour
3 tablespoons powdered whey
2 tablespoons dry Postum or other grain beverage
1 tablespoon carob powder
1 tablespoon minced onion
1½ teaspoons fine sea salt
1 tablespoon active dry yeast

continued

Put all the ingredients in the inner pan in the order listed, or in the reverse order if the manual for your machine specifies dry ingredients first and liquids last. Select the Basic Wheat cycle, Light setting (or the equivalent setting for your machine; see chart, pages 14–17). Push Start.

RUSSIAN BLACK BREAD

Variation for one 1-pound loaf

¾ cup (6 fluid ounces) water
2 teaspoons canola oil
1½ tablespoons unsulfured molasses
2 teaspoons honey
¼ teaspoon liquid lecithin
1¾ cups (8 ounces) whole wheat flour
⅓ cup (1½ ounces) rye flour
2 tablespoons powdered whey
1½ tablespoons dry Postum or other grain beverage
2 teaspoons carob powder
2 teaspoons minced onion
1 teaspoon fine sea salt
2 teaspoons active dry yeast

Put all the ingredients in the inner pan in the order listed, or in the reverse order if the manual for your machine specifies dry ingredients first and liquids last. Select the Basic Wheat cycle, Light setting (or the equivalent setting for your machine; see chart, pages 14–17). Push Start.

CHAPTER
--·-13-·--

Dairy-Free Breads

Do you realize that about 15 percent of the U. S. population is unable to tolerate lactose? Lactose, a naturally occurring sugar in all dairy products from heavy cream to cottage cheese, is easily digested by most people who secrete the enzyme lactase. Those who are lactase deficient may experience cramping or bloating after eating even just traces of a dairy product.

While not all breads are made with milk, many are. It tenderizes and conditions the dough. I understand the hardship this presents folks with lactase deficiency. I also understand the people who for philosophical reasons avoid all dairy, too. Therefore, I have gathered a few recipes that are strictly nondairy.

*Non*dairy is the only negative associated with these breads. From moist Apple Spice Bread to Salt-Free Wheat Bread, all are as flavorful as any bread in my repertoire. And all make terrific sandwiches. In fact, you will find Multigrain Buns used in as many recipes as any other bread in the book.

APPLE SPICE BREAD

Makes one 1½-pound loaf

The applesauce makes this bread moist and fruity, which is why I pair it with apples and dates for a luscious sandwich (page 102).

½ cup (4 fluid ounces) unsweetened, natural apple juice
1 cup unsweetened, natural applesauce
2 tablespoons honey
1¾ cups (8 ounces) whole wheat flour
1½ cups (7½ ounces) unbleached all-purpose flour
2 tablespoons gluten flour
1½ teaspoons fine sea salt
1 teaspoon ground cinnamon
½ teaspoon grated nutmeg
¼ cup toasted chopped walnuts
1 tablespoon active dry yeast

Put all the ingredients in the inner pan in the order listed, or in the reverse order if the manual for your machine specifies dry ingredients first and liquids last. Select the Basic Wheat cycle, Light setting (or the equivalent setting for your machine; see chart, pages 14–17). Push Start.

APPLE SPICE BREAD

Variation for one 1-pound loaf

⅓ cup (2½ fluid ounces) unsweetened, natural apple juice
⅔ cup unsweetened, natural applesauce
1½ tablespoons honey
1¼ cups (6½ ounces) whole wheat flour
1 cup (5 ounces) unbleached all-purpose flour
1½ tablespoons gluten flour
1 teaspoon fine sea salt
½ teaspoon ground cinnamon
¼ teaspoon grated nutmeg
3 tablespoons toasted chopped walnuts
2 teaspoons active dry yeast

Put all the ingredients in the inner pan in the order listed, or in the reverse order if the manual for your machine specifies dry ingredients first and liquids last. Select the Basic Wheat cycle, Light setting (or the equivalent setting for your machine; see chart, pages 14–17). Push Start.

GARDEN O' PLENTY BREAD

Makes one 1½-pound loaf

A good half-cup of pureed vegetables makes this a moist, healthful bread that tastes just right with the Tofu Cheese-Avocado (page 92) and other vegetarian sandwiches. I suggest using any cooked, cooled, and drained vegetables—carrots, broccoli, and peas are among my favorites. Sometimes I combine them. I also like to make this with cooked and cooled beets for a deep, red-colored bread. Because moisture content varies from vegetable to vegetable, you may have to adjust the amount of flour to ensure the dough is not too wet. Simply lift the lid of the bread machine after the first five or six minutes of the mixing cycle and feel the dough. If it feels very wet add flour, a tablespoon at a time, until it feels smooth and firm. Do not add too much flour.

¾ cup (6 fluid ounces) water
½ cup cooked, pureed vegetables, such as carrots, broccoli, or peas
1½ tablespoons honey
½ teaspoon liquid lecithin
3 cups (14 ounces) whole wheat flour
2 tablespoons gluten flour
1 tablespoon minced dried onion (optional)
1½ teaspoons fine sea salt
1 teaspoon dried oregano
⅛ teaspoon cayenne pepper
2 teaspoons active dry yeast

continued

Put all the ingredients in the inner pan in the order listed, or in the reverse order if the manual for your machine specifies dry ingredients first and liquids last. Select the Basic Wheat cycle, Light setting (or the equivalent setting for your machine; see chart, pages 14–17). Push Start.

GARDEN O' PLENTY BREAD

Variation for one 1-pound loaf

½ cup (4 fluid ounces) water
⅓ cup cooked, pureed vegetables, such as carrots, broccoli, or peas
1 tablespoon honey
¼ teaspoon liquid lecithin
2 cups (9½ ounces) whole wheat flour
1½ tablespoons gluten flour
2 teaspoons minced dried onion (optional)
1 teaspoon fine sea salt
½ teaspoon dried oregano
1/16 teaspoon cayenne pepper
1½ teaspoons active dry yeast

Put all the ingredients in the inner pan in the order listed, or in the reverse order if the manual for your machine specifies dry ingredients first and liquids last. Select the Basic Wheat cycle, Light setting (or the equivalent setting for your machine; see chart, pages 14–17). Push Start.

SPELT BREAD

Makes one 1½-pound loaf

Spelt is an ancient grain that is now back in fashion, partly because it can be used in place of wheat flour in breads. It is beneficial to anyone with a wheat sensitivity because it is one of the easiest of all grains to digest. I appreciate it for its flavor and its high concentration of B vitamins and minerals. Buy spelt flour in natural foods stores.

1   cup (8 fluid ounces) ice cold water
2   tablespoons honey
½   teaspoon liquid lecithin
3   cups (14 ounces) spelt flour
1½   teaspoons fine sea salt
2   teaspoons active dry yeast

Put all the ingredients in the inner pan in the order listed, or in the reverse order if the manual for your machine specifies dry ingredients first and liquids last. Select the Basic Wheat cycle, Light setting (or the equivalent setting for your machine; see chart, pages 14–17). Push Start.

SPELT BREAD

Variation for one 1-pound loaf

⅔ cup (5½ fluid ounces) ice cold water
1½ tablespoons honey
¼ teaspoon liquid lecithin
2 cups (9½ ounces) spelt flour
1 teaspoon fine sea salt
1½ teaspoons active dry yeast

Put all the ingredients in the inner pan in the order listed, or in the reverse order if the manual for your machine specifies dry ingredients first and liquids last. Select the Basic Wheat cycle, Light setting (or the equivalent setting for your machine; see chart, pages 14–17). Push Start.

NO-OIL, NO-DAIRY WHOLE WHEAT BREAD

Makes one 1½-pound loaf

Use this low-fat bread in place of other whole wheat bread for any sandwich in the book—or one of your own devising.

1 cup plus 2 tablespoons (9 fluid ounces) water
2½ tablespoons honey
1 teaspoon liquid lecithin
3 cups (14 ounces) whole wheat flour
2 tablespoons gluten flour
1½ teaspoons fine sea salt
2 teaspoons active dry yeast

Put all the ingredients in the inner pan in the order listed, or in the reverse order if the manual for your machine specifies dry ingredients first and liquids last. Select the Basic Wheat cycle, Light setting (or the equivalent setting for your machine; see chart, pages 14–17). Push Start.

NO-OIL, NO-DAIRY WHOLE WHEAT BREAD

Variation for one 1-pound loaf

¾ cup (6 fluid ounces) water
1½ tablespoons honey
½ teaspoon liquid lecithin
2 cups (9½ ounces) whole wheat flour
1½ tablespoons gluten flour
1 teaspoon fine sea salt
1½ teaspoons active dry yeast

Put all the ingredients in the inner pan in the order listed, or in the reverse order if the manual for your machine specifies dry ingredients first and liquids last. Select the Basic Wheat cycle, Light setting (or the equivalent setting for your machine; see chart, pages 14–17). Push Start.

SALT-FREE WHEAT BREAD

Makes one 1½-pound loaf

Vitamin C (ascorbic acid), in the form of crystals or a crushed vitamin C tablet, conditions bread dough so that it is soft and tender and keeps the baked bread from turning stale too quickly. I use it in this salt-free bread because the dough needs a little extra conditioning that would ordinarily be provided by added salt. As with No-Oil, No-Dairy Whole Wheat Bread (page 228), use this in place of other wheat bread for sandwiches.

1 cup plus 2 tablespoons (9 fluid ounces) water
2 tablespoons honey
1 tablespoon cider vinegar
1 teaspoon liquid lecithin
3 cups (14 ounces) whole wheat flour
1 tablespoon gluten flour
1 teaspoon ground cinnamon
¼ teaspoon ascorbic acid crystals, or 1 100 mg vitamin C tablet, crushed
2 teaspoons active dry yeast

Put all the ingredients in the inner pan in the order listed, or in the reverse order if the manual for your machine specifies dry ingredients first and liquids last. Select the Basic Wheat cycle, Light setting (or the equivalent setting for your machine; see chart, pages 14–17). Push Start.

SALT-FREE WHEAT BREAD

Variation for one 1-pound loaf

¾ cup (6 fluid ounces) water
1½ tablespoons honey
2 teaspoons cider vinegar
½ teaspoon liquid lecithin
2 cups (9½ ounces) whole wheat flour
2 teaspoons gluten flour
½ teaspoon ground cinnamon
⅛ teaspoon ascorbic acid crystals, or ½ 100 mg vitamin C tablet, crushed
1½ teaspoons active dry yeast

Put all the ingredients in the inner pan in the order listed, or in the reverse order if the manual for your machine specifies dry ingredients first and liquids last. Select the Basic Wheat cycle, Light setting (or the equivalent setting for your machine; see chart, pages 14–17). Push Start.

MULTIGRAIN BUNS

Makes 6 buns

These full-flavored buns are incredibly handy, not to mention delicious. I use them where other cooks might turn to traditional hamburger buns: for Sloppy Joes (page 53), Avocado and Mustard Grilled Chicken Sandwiches (page 66), and Salmon Burgers (page 69). I rely on powdered egg replacer to lighten and help leaven the buns, rather than liquid egg substitute used more often throughout the book. The powdered egg replacer is very effective and is sold in natural foods stores. It keeps in the kitchen cupboard—no need to refrigerate it.

1¼ cups (10 fluid ounces) water
2 tablespoons canola oil
1 tablespoon honey
1 tablespoon unsulfured molasses
½ teaspoon liquid lecithin
½ cup (1 ounce) plus 3 tablespoons Multigrain Cereal Mix (page 204)
3 cups (14 ounces) whole wheat flour
1 tablespoon powdered egg replacer
1 tablespoon gluten flour
1½ teaspoons fine sea salt
1 tablespoon active dry yeast

Put all the ingredients, except 3 tablespoons of the Multigrain Cereal Mix, in the inner pan in the order listed, or in the reverse order if the manual for your machine specifies dry ingredients first and liquids last. Select the Dough setting (or the equivalent setting for your machine; see chart, pages 14–17). Push Start. When the machine beeps after 1 hour and 20 minutes, remove the dough. Turn off the machine.

Transfer the dough to a lightly floured counter or cutting board. Cut the dough into 6 equal pieces and form each into a smooth ball. Put the balls, spaced about 4 inches apart, on a lightly oiled baking pan. Cover with a damp kitchen towel or plastic wrap. Let the dough rest for 10 minutes. Flatten each "roll" with the palm of your hand to about 1 inch thick and 3 inches wide. Brush with water and sprinkle evenly with the reserved 3 tablespoons of Multigrain Cereal Mix. Press the cereal gently into the dough so that it adhers to it. Let the buns rise for about 1 hour, or until doubled in volume.

Preheat the oven to 400°F. Bake the buns for 12 to 15 minutes or until browned. Serve hot or room temperature.

MULTIGRAIN BUNS

Variation for 4 buns

¾ cups plus 2 tablespoons (7 fluid ounces) water
1½ tablespoons canola oil
2 teaspoons honey
2 teaspoons unsulfured molasses
¼ teaspoon liquid lecithin
⅓ cup (¾ ounce) plus 2 tablespoons Multigrain Cereal Mix (page 204)
2 cups (9½ ounces) whole wheat flour
2 teaspoons powdered egg replacer
2 teaspoons gluten flour
1 teaspoon fine sea salt
2 teaspoons active dry yeast

Put all the ingredients, except 2 tablespoons of the Multigrain Cereal Mix, in the inner pan in the order listed, or in the reverse order if the manual for your machine specifies dry ingredients first and liquids last. Select the Dough setting (or the equivalent setting for your machine; see chart, pages 14–17). Push Start. When the machine beeps after 1 hour and 20 minutes, remove the dough. Turn off the machine.

Transfer the dough to a lightly floured counter or cutting board. Cut the dough into 4 equal pieces and form each into a smooth ball. Put the balls, spaced about 4 inches apart, on a lightly oiled baking pan. Cover with a damp kitchen towel or plastic wrap. Let the dough rest for 10 minutes. Flatten each "roll" with the palm of your hand to about 1 inch thick and 3 inches wide. Brush with water and sprinkle evenly with the reserved 2 tablespoons of Multigrain Cereal Mix. Press the cereal gently into the dough so that it adheres to it. Let the buns rise for about 1 hour, or until doubled in volume.

Preheat the oven to 400°F. Bake the buns for 12 to 15 minutes or until browned. Serve hot or room temperature.

A Glossary
of Ingredients

Because some of the ingredients I require may be unfamiliar, I have listed them here to explain what they are, how I use them, and, perhaps most important, where you can buy them. I have also included storage information when appropriate.

Nearly all these products are sold in natural foods stores, although many are also sold in large, chain supermarkets, coops, progressive supermarkets, and specialty stores. The best food is made from the best ingredients, which are always worth seeking out.

Ascorbic Acid is also known as vitamin C, and, when added to bread dough, conditions it for soft texture and better moisture retention, which makes the bread last a little longer than usual. I included it in only one of the recipes (Salt-Free Wheat Bread, page 230), but if you would like to try it in the others, crush one 100 milligram tablet between two spoons or use the crystals, and put it in the pan with the liquid ingredients.

Baking Powder is used to leaven desserts, and although it is a common household item, I recommend nonaluminum baking powder such as Rumford. Packaged in a red canister, Rumford is sold in both supermarkets and natural foods stores. If you buy sodium-free baking powder from a natural foods store, double the amount called for in the recipe, as these are less powerful than most commercial baking powders, including Rumford.

Bran is the outer layer of the grain. It is a good source of fiber and as such can be insoluble or soluble. Oat bran is soluble, while wheat bran is insoluble. Bran contains some B vitamins. Praised for its contribution to colon health and to maintaining healthy levels of cholesterol in the blood, bran has its limits. Too much fiber in the form of bran can interfere with the absorption of certain minerals and may even contribute to irritation of the colon. For the best balance of nutrients, bran should be left intact with the grain from which it originated, as it is in whole-grain flours. Store bran in a dry location. It contains no oils, so there is little risk of rancidity.

Brown Rice is unrefined rice that has not had the hull or bran removed and takes longer to cook than more familiar white rice. Brown rice is high in fiber, and compared to refined white rice, has a pleasing, nutty flavor. Brown rice is sold both short or long grain, and often is found in mixes with wild rice and grains. If adding brown rice to bread dough, be sure to cook the rice first.

Carob Chips are an alternative to chocolate chips in baking and snacking. They are caffeine-free, which may make them a more healthful choice, but carob chips are considered a high-fat food and are often manufactured with partially hydrogenated oils. Be sure to buy the right ones: malt-sweetened carob chips, not unsweetened, when the recipe calls for semisweet chips.

Dried Beans are a good, inexpensive source of protein and calcium. Abundant variety is available including pintos, turtles, great northern, cranberry, fava, and garbanzo. Dried beans need to be soaked in cold water for six to eight hours to break down their insoluble fiber and make then digestible. Once soaked, they should be drained and then cooked in fresh water; cooking time varies between 45 and 90 minutes, or even longer depending on the size and texture of the bean. Turn to page 143 for instructions on cooking beans. Store dried beans in a cool, dry place. They keep for eight or nine months.

Dried Fruits are dehydrated sliced or whole fruits meant to be eaten on their own as sweet snacks in trail mixes and as additions to cereals. They are also very often added to baked goods, such as bread. Raisins are perhaps the most familiar dried fruit, although apricots and dates are popular as well. Some manufacturers add sulfur dioxide to soften the texture and heighten the color of the fruit, while others treat it with potassium sorbate to combat fungus and mold. Unsulfured dried fruits are preferred and can be found in natural foods stores and some specialty markets. The law requires that this information appear on the label. Often, unsulfured dried fruits are pesticide-free as well. Dates should be refrigerated, but store other dried fruit in covered containers at room temperature.

Egg Substitute and Egg Replacer are used to avoid cholesterol, and many people use them as the main component of egg dishes. Artificial eggs, egg substitutes, and egg replacers are available in powdered and liquid forms. Products manufactured to replace eggs may contain egg white, oil, and milk or soybean products. I rely mainly on liquid egg substitute in the recipes here. It is sold in cartons in the refrigerator section of supermarkets. A scant ¼ cup of liquid egg substitute is equal to a large egg; 3 tablespoons are equal to a medium egg. They are also good for brushing on hand-formed loaves as a glaze. Liquid egg replacers should be stored in the refrigerator and used by the date indicated on the package. Dried egg replacers can be stored on the pantry shelf.

Extracts are liquid flavorings that commonly are made by blending an oily essence of a flavor (such as orange, cinnamon, or vanilla) with alcohol. Choose only natural, not imitation extracts. These are sold in natural foods stores and some supermarkets in small bottles and should be stored in a cool, dry cupboard with the caps firmly screwed on to prevent evaporation.

Gluten Flour is mainly made from gluten, the protein that reacts with yeast to give bread its characteristic rise. Like all-purpose white flour, gluten is made from the endosperm of the wheat berry, but the process is taken several steps further. The starch is removed and the remaining gluten is ground again and then combined with very finely milled white flour called patent flour. This results in a product that is approximately 50 percent gluten. Gluten flour is never used in much quantity, but I sometimes add it to whole-grain doughs to give them an extra lift. Gluten flour is also called vital wheat and high gluten flour. It is available in some supermarkets, although your best bet is a natural foods store. Buy gluten flour in small amounts and store it in a cool, dry place for several months.

Granola is a cereal made from rolled grains (oats, wheat, rye, and barley that have been minimally processed and rolled to flatten them), dried fruit, and often nuts and seeds. It was conceived by the Swiss as a healthful food providing nourishment at alpine heights. The mixture is usually sweetened with honey or maple syrup, emulsified with a little oil, and then roasted. As delicious as this sounds—and many granolas are glorious—granolas are high in fat and calories and so should be used judiciously. Granola is eaten as a snack and a breakfast cereal, and handfuls may be baked into breads for crunch and sweet flavor. Read the ingredients on the package carefully to determine the fat and calorie count, and to decide if a particular mixture will complement your recipe or appetite, or make your own. Store granola as you do breakfast cereal, but because of the oils in the nuts and grain, the mixture keeps for only a month or so. My favorite granola mixture is described in the recipe on page 145.

Herbs and Spices can be used fresh or dried to enhance the flavor of foods. Many contain valuable vitamins and minerals, and for years have been touted as having healing powers.

Dried herbs are available all year long in supermarkets, groceries, specialty stores, and natural foods stores. Although many manufacturers sell them in small plastic containers, they do best in glass. Store the herbs and spices in a dry, cool cupboard and date the jars. Replace dried leaf herbs and ground spices such as ginger and cinnamon every three to four months. Whole spices such as cardamom pods and nutmeg will keep for ten to twelve months.

Fresh herbs are easily found in most markets and during the summer months are so abundant it often does not make sense to use anything else. Choose fresh herbs such as basil, parsley, dill, cilantro, and mint with bright green color and no limp or black-tinged leaves. Wash the herbs in cool water, shake them dry, and store them in the refrigerator wrapped in a cloth towel inside a plastic bag. Use them within four or five days.

Dried herbs can be substituted for fresh by using a third as much as called for in a recipe. For example, a tablespoon of a fresh herb should be replaced with a teaspoon of a dried herb. Many of the breads in the book call for dried herbs and please use them, rather than fresh, whenever listed. Their flavor is more intense and generally they perform better in the bread machine.

Juices are the extracted liquid from fruits and vegetables. Juice is a delicious, nutritious beverage as well as a natural sweetener for dressings, sauces, desserts, cereals, and, of course, breads. Fresh juices can be made at home with a juice extractor. By using this method, they retain the maximum number of nutrients possible and supply the body with concentrated vitamins and minerals—and taste great, too. Freshly *squeezed* orange or grapefruit juice contains pulp. Citrus juice extracted from a juicer is pulp-free. Both taste wonderful. Juices can also be purchased from a natural foods store or grocery, but some nutrient loss inevitably occurs as they sit on the shelf. If you don't have a juice extractor, buy unpasteurized apple juice and fresh carrot juice from a natural foods store rather than pasteurized, crystal-clear apple juice and, perhaps, orange juice in a carton from the supermarket. During the fall, orchards sell freshly made apple cider, which is the same as unpasteurized apple juice. This is delicious and healthful, and if refrigerated will keep for four or five days. Fresh carrot juice should be consumed as soon as possible after it is made, preferably the same day.

Lecithin is a member of the phosphatide family and is used by the body to metabolize cholesterol. It is also a component of bile, which helps emulsify fats for easier utilization. Because lecithin breaks up fats and thereby prevents them from quick spoiling, it often is used as a food additive. I add it to bread doughs to condition them. Lecithin helps the gluten develop and therefore aids in the rising process and makes a big difference in the final texture and flavor of the bread. Lecithin is found abundantly in soybean foods and egg yolks and is a naturally occurring and important component of vegetable oil. For the recipes in the book calling for lecithin, use liquid lecithin, readily available in natural foods stores, or lecithin granules. The measurements are the same: a tablespoon of liquid lecithin is equal to a tablespoon of granular lecithin. The liquid is less expensive but very sticky; the granules are easier to use but may be a little harder to find. Buy it in large jars and store it at room temperature.

Neufchâtel Cheese is also called light cream cheese and has about half the calories and fat of regular cream cheese.

Nuts and Seeds are the edible kernel found inside a hard, removable shell. A powerhouse of nutrients, these versatile foods contain ample quantities of protein, oils, vitamins, and minerals. They are also high in fat. Because of the oil content, shelled nuts and seeds turn rancid quickly and should be stored in the refrigerator or freezer in a tightly sealed container.

Whenever possible, buy nuts in the shell and shell them yourself. This ensures freshness, although for amounts required in baking it can be a tedious task. The next best thing is to buy whole nutmeats, not broken pieces (which may be older and therefore closer to spoiling). Buy nuts from a natural foods or specialty store with a good turnover, which helps with the freshness factor. Be sure the nuts you buy are not salted or flavored.

Nut and Seed Butters are finely or coarsely ground nuts or seeds used as a spread or added to recipes to create sauces, dips, dressings, and loaves of bread. The most common nut butter is the all-American peanut butter; my personal choice is almond butter. Sesame paste (tahini) and walnut, cashew, and pecan butter are available, too. You can make your own nut butters in a food processor or blender, although they will not be as smooth as commercially processed butters. Natural foods stores sell unsweetened peanut butter, made fresh daily or several times a week, preferably from Valencia peanuts. This is a better choice than the type sold in supermarkets. If you buy peanut butter in a grocery store, read the label for added ingredients—do not be misled by the word *natural* in the name. Even those butters made without sugar are naturally high in calories and fat. Exotic or homemade nut and seed butters and pastes should be refrigerated.

Oils are derived from any number of seeds and vegetables. Some of the most common are corn oil, soybean oil, safflower oil, olive oil, peanut oil, and canola oil. I prefer *expeller pressed* oils, which are cool pressed and extracted with little or no solvent. They are, I believe, cleaner and more nutritious than those extracted by solvents and heat. Unrefined oils are easy to spot, as they usually are dark in color and may have sediment at the bottom of the bottle. Oils should be sold in glass bottles. Unlike their more highly processed cousins, unrefined oils have a relatively short shelf life. While most oils are sold as liquids, there are mist oils that are handy for spraying on baking pans and skillets. These, such as El Molino Canola Mist, prevent sticking but contribute very few calories to the final dish.

Undoubtedly you have heard a lot about saturated, monounsaturated, and polyunsaturated fats (and oils, which are a type of fat). These terms sound intimidating but in fact are simple to understand. Whether a fat is saturated or not has to do with its chains of hydrocarbons and how they are bonded. What we need to grasp is that saturated fats, derived mostly from animal products, appear to raise levels of serum cholesterol in the blood, which is not healthy. Unsaturated fats, both monounsaturated and polyunsaturated, help lower total cholesterol in the blood, which is good! No oil is totally unsaturated; there are always traces of saturated fats. By the same token, no oil is completely monounsaturated or polyunsaturated. But some have far more of the qualities of one than the other. Some oils are made so that they are high oleic. This means their molecules have a high percentage of double hydrocarbon bonds, which are unsaturated. High-oleic oils are primarily monounsaturated.

Polyunsaturated fats apparently lower both HDL levels ("good" cholesterol) *and* LDL levels ("bad" cholesterol), making no differentiation between the two. Monounsaturated fats lower only "bad" cholesterol levels and leave "good" cholesterol alone.

If you are still confused, remember this: oils that are primarily monounsaturated are preferred—canola, high-oleic sunflower, olive, and peanut oils are monounsaturated. Polyunsaturated oils are a close second—corn, safflower, soybean, and regular sunflower oil. Saturated fats should be avoided—butter, egg yolks, meat, cheese, and tropical oils such as coconut and palm oil.

I will not attempt to describe every type of oil on these pages, but following are four of my favorites and those I consider the best for you. Too much oil is not good for anyone—it's high in calories and fats—but a little is necessary for the fatty acids and other nutrients. Store oils in tightly capped, dark glass bottles, if possible, and keep them in a cool, dark cupboard. Depending on the type, oils turn rancid quickly if improperly stored but otherwise keep for four or five months. Some turn cloudy when refrigerated but do keep a few months longer. Let them stand at room temperature before using.

CANOLA OIL is unquestionably my favorite. It is very lightly colored and almost without flavor. A primarily monounsaturated oil and an excellent source of omega-3 fatty acids, which may help fight some cancers, its high smoking point makes it good for cooking. I use it frequently in baking. There is no "canola" grain—the oil derives its name from Canada, its country of origin where a variety of rapeseed is cultivated specifically for this healthful oil.

HIGH-OLEIC SUNFLOWER OIL is made from a sunflower hybrid and equals canola oil when it comes to monounsaturated properties. If you cannot find canola oil, use this. It is easily available in natural foods stores and some progressive supermarkets.

OLIVE OIL is unmistakably fruity in flavor and adds a special touch to many dishes and salad dressings. It is the only oil that is actually cold pressed. Olive oil is primarily monounsaturated and the best high-oleic oil money can buy. This contributes to its poor cooking qualities (it breaks down at high temperatures), although for many baking needs I find it superb.

You have heard of extra-virgin, virgin, and pure olive oils. These simply refer to the grade of oil, with the extra-virgin coming from the first, most flavorful pressing and pure olive oil from later pressings. Extra-virgin and virgin tend to taste fruitier and look greener than pure olive oil. Use these in salad dressings more than cooking.

SAFFLOWER OIL is a versatile, mild-flavored product ranging in color from pale to amber. The darker the oil, the nuttier the taste, but even the darkest safflower oil is noticeably bland. Polyunsaturated safflower oil is nearly 95 percent unsaturated fats and with 78 percent, has the highest percentage of linoleic acid of all the oils. High-oleic safflower oil, which is primarily mono-unsaturated, is appropriate for many baking needs as well as for light sautéing, pressure cooking, and in salad dressings requiring no heat at all. Both types are available in natural foods stores and progressive supermarkets. High-oleic safflower oil may be harder to find.

Salt-Free Herb and Spice Blend is the generic term for any number of products on the market that blend herbs and spices to season food without salt. Mrs. Dash is an example.

Sea Salt is made from salt water and although it is predominantly sodium chloride, it frequently contains trace minerals such as magnesium, calcium, and potassium. Sea salt is sold in supermarkets, groceries, and natural foods stores, both finely and coarsely ground. For my recipes, I use fine sea salt.

Soymilk is the liquid derived from cooked and filtered soybeans, and is a good source of phosphorous, iron, and calcium. Many people, especially those with a lactose intolerance, use it in baking and dessert making. Be sure you buy plain soymilk; some manufacturers produce sweetened soymilk flavored with chocolate, vanilla, or carob. Soymilk is most often available at natural foods stores in recyclable asceptic containers and must be refrigerated after opening.

Sweeteners include numerous alternatives to sugar. Some you can buy nearly anywhere; others are most easily found in natural foods stores. Refined white sugar is the sweetener of choice of most Americans, but I try very hard to avoid it. It provides calories with no nutritional value. Brown sugar, which is simply processed slightly differently, is no better. Neither will benefit your health in any way. Honey and syrups are just as sweet or sweeter and contribute better flavor and at least a few nutrients. When I think a recipe needs sugar for the proper consistency and texture, I use raw sugar or Sucanat (granulated, evaporated organic cane juice).

HONEY is considered the original sweetener. Surely everyone recognizes the biblical reference to the "land of milk and honey." Its flavor and color vary depending on the flowers from which the nectar was gathered. Clover honey is most common, but you can also buy orange-blossom honey, blueberry honey, raspberry honey, and so on. Honey is nearly twice as sweet as sugar, so use less when substituting it in a recipe.

MAPLE SYRUP is a pleasantly sweet product made from the boiled sap of maple trees. Maple syrup varies from golden brown to dark amber and as the grades darken, the flavor intensifies subtly. The syrup is made in the late winter and early spring when the sap runs most freely. It takes forty gallons of sap to produce one gallon of syrup, which explains in part why pure maple syrup is expensive. Maple products are also available in crystal form and as a soft spread. Be sure to buy *pure* maple syrup, not maple-flavored corn or sugar syrup. The difference in flavor, texture, and goodness is the difference between a stand of stately Vermont maple trees and a processing plant. Maple syrup is sold in specialty shops and some supermarkets. For the best quality, but it from a farmer who makes it him or herself.

MOLASSES is the liquid produced from the juice of sugarcane during white sugar refining. During processing, several grades of molasses emerge, with blackstrap being the most concentrated, bitter, and burnt tasting. If you can, look for the words *unsulfured molasses* on the label. Unsulfured molasses is available in natural foods stores, specialty shops, and some supermarkets.

RAW SUGAR is made from cane and is simply less processed than white sugar. It has no redeeming nutritional value, but some baked products turn out best when made with sugar. Raw sugar is sold in supermarkets and natural foods stores.

Tahini is a paste made from ground, hulled sesame seeds and differs from sesame butter, which is thicker and more bitter as it is made from unhulled, crushed sesame seeds. Tahini is a good source or protein, but like nut butters, it is high in calories. Try to buy tahini in natural foods stores where it is likely the product was made from sesame seeds whose hulls were removed without the aid of chemicals. Store tahini in the refrigerator.

Tamari is a high-quality soy sauce and, when authentic, contains no wheat. **Shoyu** is a similar soy-based sauce that is made from cracked, roasted wheat. The two are often mislabeled, so when buying tamari, be sure to read the label, particularly if you have a wheat allergy. Tamari and shoyu are sold in natural foods stores and Asian markets.

Tofu is a popular, versatile food made from cultured soybeans. It is sold in many supermarkets, greengrocers, Asian markets, natural foods stores, and speciality shops. While tofu is most often found in the refrigerator section of the grocery, some Asian markets sell blocks of off-white tofu from water-filled trays nestled in with the produce. The firmer the tofu, the more concentrated the nutrients—and tofu, brimming with valuble vitamins, and minerals, is a terrific source of protein. It is also low in fat and sodium. Firm and extra-firm tofu cakes are best for cooking and baking; soft, silken tofu resembles soft, young cheese and works well in dips, spreads, and salad dressings. Although it can be used in place of cheese in some recipes, tofu does not melt. Keep tofu in the refrigerator covered with water. Change the water every day or so to keep the soybean cake fresh for up to week.

Tofu Cheese is a different product from tofu. It is often flavored like cheese and can be used in place of it. Look for it in natural foods stores.

Vegetable Bouillon Cubes are similar to beef and chicken bouillon cubes and may be used as the base for vegetarian soups and sauces. Some are sodium-free, but most are not. They are sold in some supermarkets, but the most reliable source is the natural foods store. Like all bouillon cubes, these can be stored in a cool, dry cupboard.

Whey is the watery part of milk remaining after casein, its principal protein, is removed. Whey may be used as an additive to recipes in place of milk but it is *not* lactose-free. I use it in many of the bread recipes because it conditions the dough so that the final texture of the bread is firm but never hard or too chewy. Buy powdered whey in jars in natural foods stores and store it in a cool, dry cupboard.

Index

Carrot cake with Neufchâtel cheese frosting, 168–170
Catsup:
   quick homemade, 128
   spicy homemade, 129
Cereal mix, multigrain, 204
Cheddar cheese and chive bread, 190, 191
   classic chicken salad on, 29
   tuna salad on, 36–37
Cheese:
   Italian, turkey sausage, and mushroom calzone, 60–61
   Monte Cristo on basic white bread, 51–52
   and tomato on caraway rye bread, grilled, 76
   see also Cottage cheese 'n' herbs; Cream cheese; *specific cheeses*
Chicken:
   breast, poached, 137–138
   noodle soup, homemade, 157–159
   salad, classic, on cheddar cheese and chive bread, 29
   stock, 140–141
Chicken, grilled:
   avocado and mustard, on multigrain buns, 66–67
   sandwich, on old-fashioned wheat bread, 65
Chili, mountain-man, 165–166
Chips, tortilla, oven-baked, 123
Chive and cheddar cheese bread, 190, 191
   classic chicken salad, on, 29
   tuna salad on, 36–37
Chives and Neufchâtel cheese on pumpernickel bread, 108
Chuckwagon soup, 161–162
Cinnamon-raisin bread, 192, 193
   pineapple-peach-pecan sandwich on, 105

Cinnamon spread, 125
Classic chicken salad on cheddar cheese and chive bread, 29
Club sandwich, double turkey, on old-fashioned wheat bread, 31–32
Coleslaw and turkey barbecue on multigrain buns, 63–64
Complex carbohydrates, 21–24
Cooked beans, 143–144
Cookies:
   Montana oatmeal, 172–173
   peanut butter, 174–175
Corn, tomatoes, and dill, salmon salad with, on pumpernickel bread, 40
Cottage cheese 'n' herbs:
   on caraway rye bread, 88
   spread, 118
Crab Louis sandwich on basic white bread, 41–42
Cranberry spread with oranges on banana-nut bread, 106
Cream cheese:
   apricot-and-pecan, sandwich on lemon bread, 109
   herbed, on spelt bread, 101
Creamy bean spread, 122–123
Croutons, crispy, 131
Cucumber salad in yogurt cheese on basic white bread, 94–95
Curry-almond turkey salad sandwich on multigrain bread, 32–33

Date(s):
   and apples on apple spice toast, 102
   snacks, 177
   strawberries, and almond butter on oatmeal spice bread, 104

Papa's garlic-potato soup, 151–152
Peach-pineapple-pecan sandwich on
    cinnamon-raisin bread, 105
Peanut butter:
    -apple sandwich on 100 percent whole
        wheat bread, 35–36
    banana, and granola on multigrain bread,
        107
    cookies, 174–175
Pears and apple mustard, smoked turkey with,
    on Russian black bread, 33–34
Pea soup, Scandinavian split, 154–155
Pecan:
    -and-apricot cream cheese sandwich on
        lemon bread, 109
    -pineapple-peach sandwich on cinnamon-
        raisin bread, 105
Peppers, roasted red:
    with grilled tuna on pumpernickel bread,
        72–73
    with mozzarella on salt-free wheat bread,
        97–98
Pesto, 116
    mayonnaise, 115
Pineapple-peach-pecan sandwich on
    cinnamon-raisin bread, 105
Pizza sandwich on garden o' plenty bread,
    grilled, 83
Poached chicken breast, 137–138
Poached salmon fillets, 139
Potato-garlic soup, Papa's, 151–152
Pumpernickel bread, 215, 216
    Neufchâtel cheese and chives on, 108
    roasted red peppers with grilled tuna on,
        72–73
    salmon salad with corn, tomatoes, and dill
        on, 40

Quick homemade catsup, 128

Raisin-cinnamon bread, 192, 193
    pineapple-peach-pecan sandwich on,
        105
Raisin-oatmeal snack cake, 178–179
Red peppers, roasted:
    with grilled tuna on pumpernickel bread,
        72–73
    with mozzarella on salt-free wheat bread,
        97–98
Rice-turkey soup, 156–157
Roasted Italian vegetables on old-fashioned
    wheat bread, 85–86
Roasted red peppers:
    with grilled tuna on pumpernickel bread,
        72–73
    with mozzarella on salt-free wheat bread,
        97–98
Roast turkey breast, 133–134
Russian black bread, 217, 218–219
    Monterey Jack and Vidalia onion on, 89
    1990s Denver sandwich on, 49–50
    sardine sandwich on, 38–39
    smoked salmon on, with dill-herb spread,
        43
    smoked turkey with pears and apple
        mustard on, 33–34
Rye bread, caraway, 213, 214
    grilled cheese and tomato on, 76
    herbs 'n' cottage cheese on, 88

Salad:
    almond-curry turkey, sandwich on
        multigrain bread, 32–33
    classic chicken, on cheddar cheese and
        chive bread, 29

To contact George Burnett with success stories, comments, questions,
or for information about setting up a whole-grain bakery,
please write:

George Burnett
The Breadman
P.O. Box 3082
Bozeman, MT 59772

Please include a self-addressed,
stamped envelope for a response.